Presented To:

_____

By:

_____

Date:

_____

SPIRITUAL SHOCK TREATMENT

GET REAL WITH JESUS
TEEN DEVOTIONAL

by Ron Luce

ALBURY PUBLISHING
Tulsa, Oklahoma

Spiritual Shock Treatment
Get Real with Jesus Teen Devotional
ISBN 1-57778-100-7
Copyright © 1998 by Ron Luce
P. O. Box 2000
Garden Valley, Texas 75771-2000

Published by ALBURY PUBLISHING
P. O. Box 470406
Tulsa, Oklahoma 74147-0406

CONTENTS

FOREWORD

Ron Luce is one of many of the followers of Jesus Christ we've worked with over the last few years. His heart for this generation is so honest and pure that it's contagious!

I pray your reading of *Spiritual Shock Treatment* will bring you further in your walk, and help you to find God's purpose for you in His Kingdom.

Spiritual Shock Treatment is a devotional to be studied with honesty between yourself and God about every part of your life. Jesus was real; we should be real.

I know you will be blessed by this study, as I have been blessed by Ron Luce and his commitment to serving our Lord, and I pray that you too will capture a heart for this generation that is honest, pure, and contagious!

Love in Christ,
Peter Furler

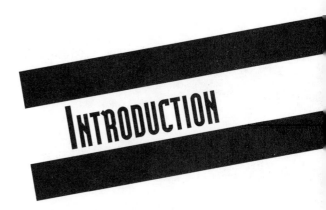

INTRODUCTION

This book is about helping you get real with God — helping you to get connected and stay connected to Jesus. There are a lot of people who have gone to church every week for years, but they're not tight with Jesus. I believe this happens because they don't spend enough time with Him — quiet time.

This devotional book gives you something to do every day in your quiet time for the next ten weeks. If you've never had a quiet time before, you probably expect to read a chapter out of the Bible and fall asleep. But as you read through this book and part of the four Gospels each day, there's going to be stuff for you to do that will cause you to reach down deep inside your heart and find out what you really believe, what is really true, why you believe it, and what are you doing with it.

I ask you to commit to go all the way through this devotional, and then go through it again and again. If you ever start feeling a little bit dry in your walk with God, or if it becomes at all monotonous or boring, this book will help you fall down on your face, cry out to God with all your heart, and get reconnected with the One Who loves you so much He gave His life for you.

Have a great time as you rip your heart wide open and allow God to do the reconstructive surgery on the inside of you to make you the man or woman of God He wants you to be. Why is He doing this? So you can change this world!

PART ONE

Get Real

It is time for you to grab hold of God

with everything you've got — and never

let go. It is time to come face-to-face

with Jesus and realize that

He's the only reason to live.

●

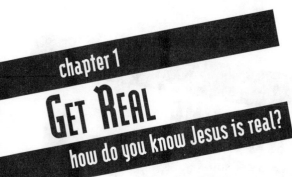

chapter 1

GET REAL
how do you know Jesus is real?

Yet I am not ashamed,
because I know whom I have believed.

2 Timothy 1:12

Day 1
. . . .

THE REALITY OF JESUS

For those of us who have been raised in church, we kind of take Jesus for granted. We've heard about Him our whole life. We've heard people talk about Him. We've heard ministers preach about Him. Our parents have told us about Him. So we've always thought He was real.

But how do you know He's real?

When Jesus came to the region of Caesarea Philippi, he asked his disciples, "Who do people say the Son of Man is?"

They replied, "Some say John the Baptist; others say Elijah; and still others, Jeremiah or one of the prophets."

"But what about you?" he asked. "Who do you say I am?"

Simon Peter answered, "You are the Christ, the Son of the living God."

Jesus replied, "Blessed are you, Simon son of Jonah, for this was not revealed to you by man, but by my Father in heaven."

Matthew 16:13-17

Jesus wasn't walking around trying to convince Peter or anyone else that He was the Son of God. He wasn't continually telling people, "I'm the Son of God. I really am, I really, really, really, really am the Son of God." In essence, Jesus was telling Peter, "I don't care about everyone else's opinion, but I do care about yours. Who do *you* think I am?"

Knowing that Jesus is the Son of God is more than just being convinced and more than just being logically persuaded. Jesus told Peter that human logic didn't convince him of this, but the Father revealed it to him. Peter's spiritual eyes were opened and he could see what was true and what was not true — what was real and what was not real. Peter had heard truth and reality from God, and that was something he was never going to forget.

The *reality* of Jesus must be the basis of our faith. He must be the basis of our Christianity. Anything else that contradicts that living, breathing reality is false — in the face of all logic, in the face of all blasphemers, in the face of everyone who mocks us and makes fun of us. If we know Jesus is real, nothing else matters.

Ask the Lord to open your eyes, just like He did Peter's, so you can see for yourself that Jesus is real. Then ask yourself, "How do I know Jesus is real?"

_____

_____

_____

_____

_____

_____

_____

CHECKLIST:

☒ Today, read Matthew 1.

☒ Spend some time praising and worshipping God.

☒ Pray over your own life and your day today.

☒ Pray for your family, friends, and those in authority.

☒ Pray for the people of the world to be saved.

☐ Ask God if He wants you to go on a mission trip next summer.

Day 2
•••••••••••••••••••••

EVIDENCE OF A CHANGED LIFE

So many people use scriptures to prove the fact that God is alive and real. They've heard Bible verses about God from Sunday school classes or in their youth group. They say all the right words and seem to talk about God as if they were close to Him. The trouble is, they sound like they are talking about a friend of a friend instead of *their* friend. They talk about God as if He's someone they've heard of rather than someone they've met. They may even say that they have a personal relationship with Him and quote Scripture to back it up, but when you look in their eyes, you don't see the evidence of a changed life.

Having a form of godliness but denying its power.

2 Timothy 3:5

People with a form of godliness but who deny God's power are sort of close to God or they sort of talk about God, but they really have no power in their life. If they had the power of God working their life, you would see some changes taking place. My question for you today is, "Do you have the evidence of a changed life?"

If Jesus is really real, then when you talk about Him, you shouldn't be talking about a friend of a friend, but *your* friend. You should be able to refer to personal experiences when He really changed your life.

You can say, "Oh yes, He's changed my life." But *how* did He change your life? Do you *think* He's changed your life because everyone's told you that when you prayed the salvation prayer He changed your life? Or do you *know* He has changed your life because when you met Him your whole heart changed, your direction changed, and your passions in life changed? Can you say that He stopped you in your tracks and you've never been the same since?

Churches are full of people who talk a lot about God and how Jesus has changed their life, but there doesn't seem to be any evidence. Every once in a while you'll come across someone who may not know all the scriptures or what the Bible has to say about certain things, but when you look in their eyes and listen to the way they talk about God, you can tell that a miracle has happened in their life. They're so happy, so changed, and so different. Man, they're so happy they're stupid sometimes!

Do you have that? Do you have the *evidence* of a changed life? Take a good look at your life today — how you talk, how you act, how you think — and write down the things Jesus has changed.

CHECKLIST:

☒ Today, read Matthew 2.

☒ Spend some time praising and worshipping God.

☒ Pray over your own life and your day today.

☒ Pray for your family, friends, and those in authority.

☒ Pray for the people of the world to be saved.

☐ Ask God if He wants you to go on a mission trip next summer.

- Given me hope when there was none - surgery, hospital, etc.
- I generally stick to my words
- I can just feel Him there, a comforting feel, like everything is going to be ok, no matter what.
- Changed the way I look at people (other races, nationalities, etc.)

Day 3
• •

GOING THROUGH THE MOTIONS

Religion can get old. I have seen so many people come down for the altar call, pray to give their life to Jesus, they are excited for a week or two, and then it gets old. Why? If Jesus is really the Lord of the universe, the Son of the living God, how could a relationship with Him get old or stale? It has to do with us as human beings. It's not God's fault: it's *our* fault. As human beings, it's easy for anything to get old to us.

Think about your relationship with your friends. If you don't constantly work to develop those friendships, they get old, boring, monotonous, and dry. Too often husbands and wives feel like they need to change and get another partner because they're bored with their spouse. Their marriage gets old because they don't keep working to keep it fresh. Just because you are married or just because you're connected by blood doesn't mean your relationship will always be fresh and real.

Human beings are prone to boredom. That's why the advertising industry always has to come out with new ads and new products, because we don't like seeing the same thing again and again. We're not machines. We're living creatures with active minds who want to be entertained, mesmerized, and tantalized.

How does a relationship with the living God get old? If we don't maintain that heart-to-heart connection with Him, where we are being honest, real, and open, then we're just going through the motions. It's our responsibility to reach down deep inside ourselves and pour out our guts to God on a regular basis. It only takes about twenty-four hours for a fresh, vibrant relationship with God to get old. Stay away from God and don't talk to Him for awhile — and all of a sudden He seems boring.

When Christians refuse to keep their hearts open, clean, and right before God, they can get in a rut in their walk with Him. They blame Him that their life isn't very exciting. They adopt a set of rules and regulations, and their Christianity becomes something totally traditional and ritualistic rather than a living, vibrant relationship with Jesus. They reduce what was once live, passionate, and exciting to a list of do's and don'ts, and the world looks at that and says, "Forget that — I don't want to be like that. I don't need more rules." But Christianity is not about rules — it's about a realness with the living God that absolutely changes your life on a regular basis.

Are you just going through the motions? Rip your heart open today and say, "God, I need to get real with You. I don't want You just in my brain or my head, I want You in the very center of my heart. I want You to be real right now, today. "

Now make a list of things you can do to keep your relationship with Jesus fresh and passionate.

Really Pray , turn to Him when I have a problem or something to thank Him for, always ask what He would do in a situation,

CHECKLIST:

- [ ] Today, read Matthew 3.
- [x] Spend some time praising and worshipping God.
- [x] Pray over your own life and your day today.
- [x] Pray for your family, friends, and those in authority.
- [x] Pray for the people of the world to be saved.
- [ ] Ask God if He wants you to go on a mission trip next summer.

15

GET REAL
how do you know Jesus is real?

Day 4
● ●

LIKE RIDING A BIKE

Have you ever met someone who acted like they really knew how to do something, but after a little while, you really started wondering if they did? Sometimes that's how it is when you talk to someone who says they're a Christian. They're kind of a Christian in their head, but have they really met Jesus? They say they have a "personal relationship" with Him, they say they've gone to church their whole life, they say they've prayed the salvation prayer, but the way they talk about God makes you wonder if they've really ever met Him.

How would it be if you were trying to tell someone how to ride a bike, having never ridden one yourself? You've seen people ride a bike, you've talked to other people who have ridden bikes, you've read books about riding bikes, but you've never ridden one yourself. Yet somehow you think you know enough to tell someone else how to ride a bike. That's what some Christians are like. They don't know what the Bible says about a personal relationship, but they talk about a personal relationship. They may even know scriptures about having a personal relationship, but have they ever really met God?

Sometimes it bugs me when people say they have a *personal relationship* with Jesus. Think about it for a second. If you're close friends or best friends with Joe, do you say, "I have a *personal relationship* with Joe?" No — you say, "He's my best friend." But we couch our Christianity in words like *personal relationship* so we can feel like we have something with God when maybe there's not much there at all.

We look at praying a prayer of salvation in such a casual way. With our hands in our pockets, we scuff our feet and say, "Yeah, I sort of have this relationship with God," but have we ever really met Him? Could we *accidentally* meet Michael Jordan and say, "I think I have a personal relationship with him"? If we had ever met Michael Jordan, there would be no question in our mind who we met and how well we knew him.

If you have really met Jesus, you won't be saying, "Yeah, I have a personal relationship," in a real drone kind of voice. No, the time you met the King of kings and Lord of lords will stick out in your brain for the rest of your life! It will have riveted your heart to His heart and you'll remember forever that that was the day in history that changed your life forever. From that moment on, you were never the same.

But as many as received him, to them gave he power to become the sons of God, even to them that believe on his name.

John 1:12 KJV

We say we have received the Lord in our heart, but what does that really mean? Do we somehow let Him come inside? The Greek meaning of the word **receive** means to get a hold of, to seize, to obtain, and to take hold. (See James Strong's, *The Exhaustive Concordance of the Bible* (Nashville: Abingdon, 1890), "Greek Dictionary of the New Testament," #2983.) The point is, we don't *sort of* receive the Lord, and we can't *sort of* have a relationship with Him. We are to take hold of Jesus.

Think about the bicycle example. Jesus doesn't want us to be *talking* about the bike, He wants us to *ride* the bike. He doesn't want us to *tell* people it's a really neat thing to *have* a relationship, He wants us to *have* a relationship. He wants us to get connected, to grab hold of Him and not let go.

Have you ever *seized* Jesus? Have you taken hold of Him, or are you kind of talking about Him just like you would be talking about a bike you've never ridden? Today is the day to get on the bike! Today is the day to seize Him, to grab a hold of Jesus with every bit of energy you have, to wrap your life around Him and never let go. Describe the time you seized Jesus — even if it is right now.

> -At church camp. It was when they were calling for us to come forward. The previous year I didn't go up, but this year I could feel something (GOD) pulling me up. I felt all tingley and joyful.

CHECKLIST:

☑ Today, read Matthew 4.

☒ Spend some time praising and worshipping God.

☒ Pray over your own life and your day today.

☒ Pray for your family, friends, and those in authority.

☒ Pray for the people of the world to be saved.

☐ Ask God if He wants you to go on a mission trip next summer.

GET REAL
how do you know Jesus is real?

Day 5
. . . .

HANGING ONTO SHIRTTAILS

How do you know Jesus is real? Think about it. Many people believe Jesus is real because their parents have always told them He was real.

Your pastor tells you He's real, the youth pastor tells you He's real, the preachers on the radio and television say Jesus is real. How could all these people be wrong? He must be real. As a result we have many people who believe because other people believe. But they don't believe Jesus is real because they *know* He's real, they just assume that it's true because everyone has always said it's true.

It's time for you to think about it and come to that realization on your own.

Sometimes we don't question what our parents or pastor believe is true, but in order for us to really get connected and stay connected to Jesus, we've got to question it. Is this Christianity thing really true?

Do you believe Jesus is real because *you know* it's true, or do you believe it because someone else says it's true? Think about that carefully, because your answer could determine whether you have a dry, boring, monotonous, stale, stagnant, petrified Christian life, or whether you have a life-changing encounter with the living God.

Are you hanging on the spiritual shirttails of your parents and others? Are you a believer in this stuff because everyone says you're supposed to believe it, or do you believe that Jesus is real because you know deep down in your heart of hearts that Jesus is real and He has changed your life? Right now is the time to slam on the brakes and ask yourself, "How do I know He's real?" Is He real to you or are you relying on someone else's faith?

How do you know if you are walking in your own faith rather than resting on someone else's faith? When you discover Jesus is real for yourself, there's nothing anyone else can do to provoke you into rejecting Him, doubting Him, or making you not want to follow Him. You've discovered the only One Who really is real.

Examine yourself right now to see if there is anything anyone could say or do, or if there is anything that could happen, which would cause you to doubt Jesus is real. If there isn't, great!

But if there is anyone or anything that could persuade you to turn away from Jesus, then I'm telling you right now you haven't really met Him. Get on your face and tell Him everything — your doubts, your fears, your hurts, your dreams.

Doubts _____

_____

Fears _____

_____

Hurts _____

_____

Dreams_____

_____

Ask Him to come into your heart and change your life forever. I guarantee you, He'll show up and you'll never be the same.

God's Answers_____

_____

_____

_____

_____

_____

_____

CHECKLIST:

☒ Today, read Matthew 5.

☒ Spend some time praising and worshipping God.

☒ Pray over your own life and your day today.

☒ Pray for your family, friends, and those in authority.

☒ Pray for the people of the world to be saved.

☐ Ask God if He wants you to go on a mission trip next summer.

GET REAL
how do you know Jesus is real?

Day 6
. . . .

CEREBRAL, SINCERE,
BUT NOT SAVED?

We've heard it said, "If you just accept Jesus Christ, you'll be saved." But what does that mean? Do you know the Bible never asks us to *accept* Christ? It's not in Scripture. When we use the words "accept Christ," it sounds like we're doing Jesus a favor. *Well, Jesus really doesn't have much acceptance in this world and maybe He has poor self-esteem, so we need to accept Him.*

You're a passive Christian if you say, "I'll accept Jesus as long as I don't have to change anything in my life. I'll just kind of sit here and accept Him."

For whosoever shall call upon the name of the Lord shall be saved.

Romans 10:13 KJV

Passive Christianity is believing what the preacher and the Bible say in our head and sincerely thinking it's true, but never committing to it. Our goal is not just to believe, but to believe so much that we call on the name of the Lord so we'll be saved — all day, every day. We believe it so much that we commit our entire life to Him.

What does it really mean to become a Christian? Accepting Christ is something God never asked anyone to do. I think what most people mean is that by accepting Christ they want to accept forgiveness, but the way we get forgiveness is by reaching out towards Jesus and saying, "I give You my life." You'll find many people who believe everything the Bible says with their mind, but does that mean they are really saved? Have they given their life to Jesus and actually allowed Him to take over?

The Bible says in Luke 6:46, **Why do you call me, "Lord, Lord," and do not do what I say?** Many will very sincerely call Jesus Lord, but they don't do what He asks them to do. How many people go to church every Sunday and call Jesus their Lord, but they really don't do what He asks?

Jesus asks for every piece of us, not just our brain, but our heart, our life, our soul, our passion, and every ounce of who we are. He wants to direct our life to where He's the center and we are not. That goes beyond just believing in our head. Commitment to Jesus truly changes our heart and the direction of our life.

What am I really saying here? If you've given your life to Jesus and He is really real to you and the center of your being, are you going to go around cussing, getting drunk or high on drugs, or having sex outside of marriage? Are you going to gossip about someone one minute and then act like they're your friend the next? Are you going to cheat on a test at school or steal a CD from the store? Would you lie to your parents that you weren't feeling well, so you wouldn't have to go to school?

When you really meet Jesus and give your life to Him, you want more than anything to please Him, to do what He says to do in His Word and to follow the leading of the Holy Spirit inside you.

Has He really changed your life? Write down some major changes that have taken place.

_____

_____

_____

_____

_____

_____

_____

If you cannot come up with anything, you probably haven't truly surrendered all of yourself to Him. Do that right now!

CHECKLIST:
• • • • • • • • • • • • • •

☒ Today, read Matthew 6 and 7.

☒ Spend some time praising and worshipping God.

☒ Pray over your own life and your day today.

☒ Pray for your family, friends, and those in authority.

☒ Pray for the people of the world to be saved.

☐ Ask God if He wants you to go on a mission trip next summer.

GET REAL
how do you know Jesus is real?

Day 7
. . . .

CONVINCED BUT NOT CONVERTED?

When I was sixteen years old and ran into Jesus, I knew I would never be the same again. I felt the presence of God in the church, and when I gave my life to Him, I went totally fanatical after Jesus with all my heart. I knew I was changed. I was different and I didn't care what anyone thought of me. I wasn't just convinced in my head, I knew in my heart He was real. I had given my life to Jesus and, as a result, He changed my heart and I've never been the same since.

What I just described does not happen to those who just mentally agree with everything that's in the Bible. They are convinced that being a Christian is really the right way to go because of what someone told them, maybe a preacher or a friend. But are they *converted*? Although they agree with everything the preacher says or everything you would tell them the Bible says, you can't look in their eyes and see a radical, fanatical change.

Maybe they haven't really given their life completely over to Jesus.

> You believe that there is one God. Good! Even the demons believe that — and shudder.

James 2:19

Even demons believe that Jesus is alive and real! They're even scared of Him, but obviously they haven't given their lives to Jesus or been changed in any way. So the question to ask yourself at the end of this week is this, "Do I just believe it in my head, or has Jesus really changed my life? Am I a mental Christian or a changed Christian? Am I cerebral or am I really saved? Am I convinced or converted?"

If you've been *convinced* because of some preacher, then someone else will come and convince you of something else. If a preacher convinces you to live for God, then the world or peer pressure can convince you not to live for God. The cycle continues on and on. Another revival or evangelist comes along and convinces you to live for God — until the world convinces you otherwise.

It's not a matter of logic. It's a matter of "Jesus is Lord" being so real that you give your life to Him and it totally changes. He changes you from the inside out. You get a brand new heart and a brand new life. You almost can't describe it in human words, because it's a miracle that happens inside of you when you are converted.

This is the idea of being converted: If you convert something electrical from 120 volts to 220 volts, you have converted it to a different power source. When you're converted to Jesus, your power source changes. You're changed on the inside and you have power from God to live your life.

Up to now you may have believed the Bible in your head, but you don't really think your life has been changed. Or maybe you once had that reality in your heart, but the fire has gone out. Now it's just a head trip. If you know it's true in your head and you want Jesus to change your life, right now is the time to say, "I'm not gonna go one day further without being changed."

Slam on the brakes of your life and say, "Jesus, I need You to be real to me. I need You to change my life."

Would you reach down to the deepest part of your heart and pray these words? Make them real between you and Jesus.

Lord Jesus, I'm tired of just knowing in my head that You're real. I need You to change my life. I ask You now to come and take control. I give You every part of my heart, every part of my soul, every part of my mind, and every part of my life. It's no longer me in charge, but You. Change me from the inside out. Give me a brand new heart. Do a miracle inside of me. I commit to passionately follow You every minute of every day for the rest of my life. You're the Lord, You're the King, You're my boss, and I want no one else. Change me right now. Make me a new person. In Jesus' name I pray, amen.

When you're changed forever you won't ever wonder, *Did I really get saved? Am I really different?* When you meet the living God, you *know* you are changed.

Therefore, if anyone is in Christ, he is a new creation; the old has gone, the new has come!

2 Corinthians 5:17

Pause for a second and realize what's just happened in your life. Write down the moment you felt changed and all the changes that have taken place since that time.

_____

_____

_____

_____

_____

_____

Then praise and worship Him for all He's done and all He's going to do in your life.

CHECKLIST:
• • • • • • • • • • • •

☑ Today, read Matthew 8 and 9.

☐ Spend some time praising and worshipping God.

☑ Pray over your own life and your day today.

☑ Pray for your family, friends, and those in authority.

☑ Pray for the people of the world to be saved.

☐ Ask God if He wants you to go on a mission trip next summer.

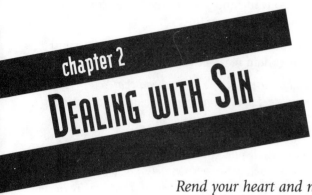

chapter 2

DEALING WITH SIN

Rend your heart and not your garments.
Return to the Lord your God, for he is gracious
and compassionate, slow to anger and abounding
in love, and he relents from sending calamity.

Joel 2:13

Day 1

STAY HONEST — STAY CONNECTED

The next four chapters are spiritual checklists for you to test your heart. Commit to have your quiet time every day and keep your relationship with Jesus Christ alive. It will prevent you from falling back into a mental kind of Christianity. Don't accidentally do what us humans do best — go back into automatic pilot where Christianity becomes an old, monotonous routine.

No one else can measure from the outside what takes place on the inside, but there are a lot of ways *you* can measure what's going on inside you. I challenged you last week: Do you just mentally agree with all the Bible says, or did Jesus really come inside your heart and change it? Your answer to that question will tell you a lot about what's happening inside you.

Go through these spiritual checklists over the next several weeks and *be very honest with yourself.* Only if you're going to get really honest with yourself and honest before God will you have a face-to-face encounter with Jesus that will change your life and continue to change your life. But if you go through this book, just do it in your brain, and refuse to open up your heart, it's just going to be another mental exercise and you'll end up going through the motions for years to come as a mental Christian. Then you'll always be wondering why some people are so thrilled and so changed, but you just kind of believe and don't see any change.

Right now I want you to commit to be honest before God. For once in your life be honest and transparent before Him in dealing with the deepest personal issues in your life. You're not doing this because your friends are doing it, or because it's a neat Christian thing to do, but because *you* want to have a life-changing encounter with God.

The truth is, if you are not going to be honest in your quiet time with God, you will never be honest with anyone else or in any other situation. You'll lie to yourself, to God, to your family, and to your friends. Your whole life will become a sham and a joke. That's why I'm getting in your face right now to dig deep and tell the truth.

If there is any area of your life where you are not being honest — with yourself, with God, with your parents, with your teachers, with your employer, with your friends — confess it to God right now and get it straight.

_____

_____

_____

Make the commitment that from this day on you are going to be honest.

CHECKLIST:
● ● ● ● ● ● ● ● ● ● ● ● ●

- ☒ Today, read Matthew 10.

- ☒ Spend some time praising and worshipping God.

- ☒ Pray over your own life and your day today.

- ☒ Pray for your family, friends, and those in authority.

- ☒ Pray for the people of the world to be saved.

- ☐ Ask God if He wants you to go on a mission trip next summer.

DEALING WITH SIN

Day 2
● ●

TELL IT LIKE IT IS

When the woman saw that the fruit of the tree was good for food and pleasing to the eye, and also desirable for gaining wisdom, she took some and ate it. She also gave some to her husband, who was with her, and he ate it.

Then the eyes of both of them were opened, and they realized they were naked; so they sewed fig leaves together and made coverings for themselves.

Then the man and his wife heard the sound of the Lord God as he was walking in the garden in the cool of the day, and they hid from the Lord God among the trees of the garden.

But the Lord God called to the man, "Where are you?"

He answered, "I heard you in the garden, and I was afraid because I was naked; so I hid."

Genesis 3:6-10

Adam and Eve were ashamed that they had disobeyed God by eating the forbidden fruit, and Adam's initial response was to try to hide his sin. When he knew he had done wrong and his heart wasn't right with God, he ran from Him.

He who conceals his sin does not prosper.

Proverbs 28:13

If you believe in your head mentally that Jesus is good and the Bible's right, but your heart isn't right with God, your initial response is to try to cover up your sin, pretend it's not there, and pretend that God doesn't even know about it.

Adam knew God was real. He had spent a lot of time with Him. Yet he was ashamed of what he had done and his heart wasn't right. And the worst part about his sin was that he wasn't connected to God anymore.

We have lots of Christians sitting in church every week pretending they're not sinning. They're getting drunk on Saturday night and going to church on Sunday — pretending that they're goodie-two-shoes type people. But sin always disconnects them from God. So they wonder why God doesn't seem real to them.

God doesn't play games with sin, because it's a killer.

For the wages of sin is death.

Romans 6:23

We have to check our own hearts. What is our initial response when we blow it? Do we try to make sure other people don't see it? Do we lie to ourselves by believing God doesn't see it — or care? Do we go on and sin as long as we can until we get into such a mess that only God can help — and then we repent?

How do you respond when someone catches you sinning or when the Holy Spirit convicts you in your heart? Do you try to deny it? Do you say it didn't really happen or excuse it away? Or do you just come clean?

If you see evidence of denial in your life, get honest with yourself and with God right now! Commit to be different than Adam. Tell Jesus everything — the good, the bad, and the ugly. If you open your heart to Him, he'll cleanse you, heal you, and make you whole.

_____

_____

_____

_____

_____

_____

_____

CHECKLIST:

☑ Today, read Matthew 11.

☑ Spend some time praising and worshipping God.

☑ Pray over your own life and your day today.

☐ Pray for your family, friends, and those in authority.

☒ Pray for the people of the world to be saved.

☐ Ask God if He wants you to go on a mission trip next summer.

DEALING WITH SIN

Day 3

BE LIKE ZACCHAEUS

Jesus entered Jericho and was passing through.

A man was there by the name of Zacchaeus; he was a chief tax collector and was wealthy.

He wanted to see who Jesus was, but being a short man he could not, because of the crowd.

So he ran ahead and climbed a sycamore-fig tree to see him, since Jesus was coming that way.

When Jesus reached the spot, he looked up and said to him, "Zacchaeus, come down immediately. I must stay at your house today."

So he came down at once and welcomed him gladly.

Luke 19:1-6

Zacchaeus' attitude toward Jesus was correct. He was curious and interested, so he climbed a tree to try to get a glimpse of Jesus. When Jesus invited Himself over to Zacchaeus' house, he said, "Great, come on!"

Before you hear what Jesus wants to do in your life, you have to ask yourself, "Do I have Zacchaeus' attitude? Am I curious and interested, or do I really think it's just the same old thing, more of that Jesus stuff and whatever from the Bible?"

Is your heart saying, "Man if this is real, I want more of it. If He is really the Son of God, I want to get up in the tree and see Him. I want to check Him out — and if He wants to come over, I'm gonna let Him come over!"

Too many people sit in church without the slightest interest or curiosity about God. They don't want more of God and they don't care anymore. They've become calloused to truth. They think they've heard it all before and no one can tell them anything new.

When a person has no interest in the truth of God's Word, there is nothing the Holy Spirit can tell them. Because it's the truth that sets people free, and they have turned their back on truth, they cannot get free of sin or anything else. As a result, instead of dealing with sin correctly by confessing and repenting, they just try to hide it and cover it up. Their attitude towards God is condescending and patronizing. They think, *Okay, maybe I'll give Jesus a break and give Him a little of my attention.*

Listen, they're not doing *Him* any favors! He doesn't need them, they need Him! Without Him, they have no power to overcome sin or get free of all the trash that the world and the devil have put on them.

Do you have the attitude of Zacchaeus? Are you curious to know more about God and interested in discovering the truths in His Word? If you are, then you will break through and you will get something real from God today.

If you don't have the attitude of Zacchaeus, I'll be real honest with you, this day will not do much for you. So jerk yourself out of this deep sleep you're in, open your eyes, splash the cool water of God's Word on them, and get a curiosity and passion to know God!

Write down at least five questions you would ask Jesus if He was standing right in front of you, in the flesh, right now. Then get your Bible or talk to your youth pastor or pastor about finding those answers. Believe me, Jesus knows the answers!

1. What do you think about me wanting to have someone special?

2. What happens to people who are mentally challenged, so never really have a chance to love / understand / know God?

3. _____

CHECKLIST:
• • • • • • • • • • • • • •

☑ Today, read Matthew 12.

☑ How do you respond to sin?

☑ Spend some time praising and worshipping God.

☑ Pray over your own life and your day today.

☑ Pray for your family, friends, and those in authority.

☑ Pray for the people of the world to be saved.

☐ Ask God if He wants you to go on a mission trip next summer.

4. _____

5. _____

DEALING WITH SIN

Day 4
● ●

DO THE ZACCHAEUS THING

So he ran ahead and climbed a sycamore-fig tree to see him, since Jesus was coming that way.

When Jesus reached the spot, he looked up and said to him, "Zacchaeus, come down immediately. I must stay at your house today."

So he came down at once and welcomed him gladly.

All the people saw this and began to mutter, "He has gone to be the guest of a 'sinner.'"

But Zacchaeus stood up and said to the Lord, "Look, Lord! Here and now I give half of my possessions to the poor, and if I have cheated anybody out of anything, I will pay back four times the amount."

Luke 19:4-8

Zacchaeus had a curious and hungry heart. He wanted to learn more and find out if Jesus was for real. So when Jesus wanted to come to his house, he was glad about it. Now Zacchaeus had heard Jesus preach and tell a few parables, but as

dealing with sin
● ●
do the Zacchaeus thing

they were hanging out together, all of a sudden Zacchaeus stood up and said, "I'm getting rid of half of my stuff. I'm gonna give to the poor and if I cheated anyone, I'm gonna pay them back four times what I took."

Think about the significance of that. Jesus didn't give an altar call. He didn't ask Zacchaeus to repent. Jesus didn't even get in his face. He was just being the Son of God. He was being Who He was — a living representation of God Himself. When Zacchaeus realized who Jesus was, his initial response was to get rid of sin, not cover it up. He didn't try to pretend he hadn't stolen anything or hadn't ripped people off. He said, "Man, I want my heart and my life right. I want the garbage to be out of me. I want to be clean."

You know what I'm saying about Jesus is true! When you're in His presence your initial response is to get rid of the garbage in your life. When Jesus is real, no one has to preach at you to clean up your life. You just know Jesus is real and you want to please Him.

If your initial response is not like Zacchaeus', then is Jesus really real in your life or is He just in your head? Are you really opening up to Him — telling him your whole life — and seeking to be in His presence?

If you're like Adam, trying to cover everything up, then maybe you believe in Jesus and you know He's there, but your heart is not opened wide to Him. When you're really connected to Jesus, you want to stay right before Him. You want to maintain a right relationship. It's like when you break your best friend's heart — maybe you've put them down or pushed them away from you — you feel so grieved and so bad that the first thing you want to do is go and make that thing right.

Look in your heart and ask yourself, "Is my heart like Zacchaeus'? Am I ready to drop everything, come running to Jesus, and do whatever it takes to make things right?" Zacchaeus knew Jesus was the Messiah and he did what his heart told him to do was right, even though Jesus hadn't even asked him about the sin in his life.

If we confess our sins, he is faithful and just and will forgive us our sins and purify us from all unrighteousness.

1 John 1:9

It's time for you to do what you know your heart is telling you to do — get rid of the garbage by asking God to forgive you and letting Jesus clean out your life. Make your heart agree with your brain — do the Zacchaeus thing today. Write down anything standing between you and God and make it right today.

_____

_____My sin._____

_____

CHECKLIST:
• • • • • • • • • • • • • • • •

☑ Today, read Matthew 13.

☑ How do you respond to sin?

☑ Spend some time praising and worshipping God.

☑ Pray over your own life and your day today.

☑ Pray for your family, friends, and those in authority.

☑ Pray for the people of the world to be saved.

☐ Ask God if He wants you to go on a mission trip next summer.

DEALING WITH SIN

Day 5

YOUR RESPONSE TO SIN

In checking your heart to see if you're like Adam (running and hiding) or Zacchaeus (coming clean) when you sin, ask yourself this, "Does someone need to confront me on every little thing in order for me to repent?"

"If your brother sins against you, go and show him his fault, just between the two of you. If he listens to you, you have won your brother over.

"But if he will not listen, take one or two others along, so that 'every matter may be established by the testimony of two or three witnesses.'

"If he refuses to listen to them, tell it to the church; and if he refuses to listen even to the church, treat him as you would a pagan or a tax collector.

"I tell you the truth, whatever you bind on earth will be bound in heaven, and whatever you loose on earth will be loosed in heaven."

Matthew 18:15-18

When we see a brother or sister involved in sin, Jesus said we are to go and confront them. If that doesn't bring about change, then we're to bring them to another brother or sister. If that still doesn't work, we're to bring them before the church. For many people, if you point out the sin in their life, their response is, "Wait a minute, I didn't do that," or "It's not *my* fault," or "Who are you to talk, are you perfect?" Is that you? Do you try to deny it like Adam did?

Other times someone will say to us, "Hey, why are you acting like that?" We'll know what we are doing is wrong, but we won't change our life. We won't decide to change that part of us. Even if people mention it — maybe the youth pastor or our parents will talk to us about an area of sin in our life — we still don't really change.

How many times do you need to be confronted about something in your life before you deal with it? If you're waiting for people to confront you again and again, or if your preacher has to preach ten sermons on why not to cuss before you start thinking, *Maybe I shouldn't cuss,* maybe you need to ask yourself, "Is Jesus really real to me or is this just in my head?"

If your parents have to tell you a hundred times not to scream at your little brother, you need to ask yourself once again, "What is my response to sin? When I sin do I need people to beat me up before I deal with it?"

Your response to sin can indicate if this Christianity thing is just in your head or if it's really in your heart. If your heart is tender towards God, you're going to want to change to be more like Him. At the least chance you are doing the wrong thing, you'll straighten yourself out and do what's right in order to stay connected with Him.

Look at your life and get down to the reality of it — your attitudes, actions, and behavior. If there is any sin between you and God, confess it. Don't let anything grieve your heavenly Father's heart or come between you and Him.

Attitudes that need work:

- Sometimes feel I can't do something

Actions to be taken:

Behavior that needs to be changed:

Lustfulness

CHECKLIST:
● ● ● ● ● ● ● ● ● ● ● ● ● ● ● ●

☑ Today, read Matthew 14.

☑ How do you respond to sin?

☑ Spend some time praising and worshipping God.

☑ Pray over your own life and your day today.

☑ Pray for your family, friends, and those in authority.

☑ Pray for the people of the world to be saved.

☐ Ask God if He wants you to go on a mission trip next summer.

DEALING WITH SIN

Day 6

CONVICTION OF THE HOLY SPIRIT

Yesterday we talked about people confronting us and getting in our face about sin in our lives, and sometimes God may use that. But God really wants us to be so in tune with Him that when He speaks something to our heart — an area that we need to change to be more like Him — we listen to Him and straighten up immediately. If we would change when the Holy Spirit convicts us, maybe we wouldn't have to go through embarrassing confrontations with people.

You can tell when the Holy Spirit is convicting you. Jesus said in John 16:8 that the Holy Spirit would come and convict the world of sin. God is constantly trying to refine our heart, our mind, and our life to be more pure. As He convicts us of things in our heart, we have to look at our first response.

Some people say, "Well, no one else knows I'm doing this, so it's really no big deal. It's not harming anyone. I'm okay. That was just my mind telling me it was wrong." No, it was the Holy Spirit saying, "You know what, I want to make you more like

Jesus." But when He begins to convict your heart of something and you put it off, you get a little bit harder and a little bit harder each time you ignore Him.

Some people think as long as other people don't see them sinning, then they're not doing anything wrong. But if you want a face-to-face encounter with God, you've got to make sure your heart is completely clean and completely right all the time. You can't have the attitude of, *Hey, I haven't done anything really wrong. I haven't robbed any banks today. I guess I'm doing pretty good.*

There's a level of purity and a level of holiness that goes far deeper in your heart than what anyone will ever see. That is what God's wanting to get to on a regular basis — to reach way down deep into your heart to constantly refine it and purify it. That's what keeps you real with Him.

So I strive always to keep my conscience clear before God and man.

Acts 24:16

Paul lived with a clean heart and a clean life. Whenever his heart was convicted, he immediately repented and got things right. Living this way doesn't mean that you're perfect, but you can have a "perfect" heart. If you will constantly let the Holy Spirit clean it out and refine it, He can develop a pure and perfect heart within you.

This is not to say that you should struggle with the same sin for the rest of your life! Once God has forgiven you, He forgets all about it. After God convicts your heart about something and you repent and He cleanses you, you'll be stronger in that area and go on. Then He will convict your heart about something else and you'll get stronger and stronger in that area. So you go from glory to glory, becoming more and more like Jesus every day for the rest of your life.

As you continue to read your Bible and pray today, ask God, "What is it about my life You want me to pray about? In what areas of my life do You want me to become more like You?"

Then just listen. As thoughts come up from your spirit, that's the Holy Spirit beginning to deal with you about certain areas, attitudes or the way you talked to someone yesterday. Ask Him to give you wisdom and direction about how to deal with anything He shows you if you don't know.

Purpose in your heart that your first response to the Holy Spirit's conviction is repentance. When someone talks to you about sin, be one who humbles himself and immediately repents. You are on the right path to having a very real encounter with Jesus today!

List the times in the past few days that you know the Holy Spirit has convicted you. Then next to each one write down what you intend to do about them.

CONVICTION   ACTION

CHECKLIST:

☑ Today, read Matthew 15 and 16.

☑ How do you respond to sin?

☑ Spend some time praising and worshipping God.

☑ Pray over your own life and your day today.

☑ Pray for your family, friends, and those in authority.

☑ Pray for the people of the world to be saved.

☐ Ask God if He wants you to go on a mission trip next summer.

DEALING WITH SIN

Day 7

RESPONDING WITH REPENTANCE

As we come to the conclusion of this chapter on sin, I want to make sure you're not just a convinced Christian, but that you are really converted and really changed.

- Are you holding on to sin?

- What is your first response when someone confronts you about sin in your life?

- What is your response when you realize you're involved in some kind of sin?

- Do you justify your sin or do you seek to rip it out of your heart as fast as you possibly can?

Now's the time to decide what kind of Christian you're going be.

Maybe you're holding on to sin right now. It could be secret sins, big sins, or little sins. It really doesn't matter. It could be things that people have talked to you about or things that God has talked to you about. Right now is the time to make sure your heart and your life are completely pure before God.

If your walk with God has been dry, monotonous, and boring because you are messing around with sin, right now is the time to rip your heart wide open and say, "God, I want You to examine every motive of my heart and every part of my life." It's time to do the Zacchaeus thing. It's time to drop everything and say, "Lord, I'm coming to follow You with every part of my life."

Take time right now to clean out everything. Purpose in your heart that this is the kind of Christian you're going to be. Don't just get your heart cleaned out one time and think that's all you have to do. Make it a daily habit of letting the waterfall of God's cleansing grace wash your life. Every time you feel in your heart that you've done something wrong, be like Zacchaeus. Get on your knees, get on your face, and say, "God, here I am all over again."

Get on your knees right now and pray this prayer with me. Please don't just pray this with your head, but think about the meaning behind the words you're about to say to your Lord, because this is going to be a pivotal point in your intimacy with Jesus for the rest of your life. If you want Him to be real to you, you've got to make sure that the position and the attitude of your heart is one that is eagerly wanting more of Him. Determine to get rid of whatever garbage you have to make things right with Him.

Lord Jesus, I choose to do the Zacchaeus thing. I choose to lay down every sin, every temptation, every thought, and every action that doesn't line up with Your Word. I know there are things people have talked to me about and You have spoken to my heart about that I need to clean out right now. I give them to You. I repent. Forgive me, Lord. I commit to get strong in these areas so they're not a hassle to me for the rest of my life. As a result, I'll become a stronger man or woman of God for You. I commit to be this kind of a Christian — to respond to Your conviction with repentance so I can get strong in that area and represent You well. In Jesus' name I pray, amen.

I want to encourage you to use this checklist every day in your quiet time:

Is my heart open? _____

_____

Is there anything God's wanting to convict me of? _____

_____

Is there sin in my life? _____

_____

Is there any garbage I did yesterday that I need to stop doing?

_____

_____

_____

_____

If you answer these questions honestly and make sure your heart is right every day, your relationship with Jesus will be fresh every day. It will be intimate because you're not holding anything back from Him. Then watch out, because you'll never experience the monotony of a petrified relationship with Jesus Christ again!

CHECKLIST:
• • • • • • • • • • • • • • •

☐ Today, read Matthew 17 and 18.

☒ How do you respond to sin?

☐ Spend some time praising and worshipping God.

☒ Pray over your own life and your day today.

☐ Pray for your family, friends, and those in authority.

☐ Pray for the people of the world to be saved.

☐ Ask God if He wants you to go on a mission trip next summer.

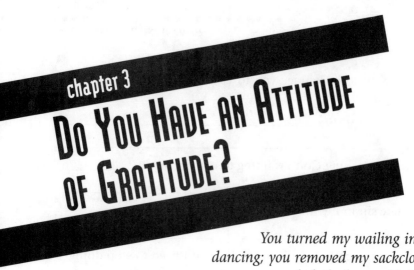

chapter 3
Do You Have an Attitude of Gratitude?

*You turned my wailing into
dancing; you removed my sackcloth
and clothed me with joy,*

*That my heart may sing to you and not be silent.
O Lord my God, I will give you thanks forever.*

Psalm 30:11,12

*Praise the Lord. Give thanks to the Lord,
for he is good; his love endures forever.*

Psalm 106:1

Day 1

THE GIFT OF FORGIVENESS

We've been talking about how to make sure you have a real connection with Jesus. It's not just a mundane ritual called Christianity that you're a part of, but eternal life has been breathed into your heart by the very living Jesus Himself.

Continue to follow the first checklist in chapter two last week to make sure you're not just a mental, shallow Christian. Ask yourself every day in your quiet time, "Lord, is there any sin I need to deal with? If so, I'm gonna fall on my knees and repent right away and get my heart clean."

This week your second checklist asks this, "Are you really grateful that you're forgiven?"

Any well-meaning Christian would say, "Well, of course, Ron, I'm grateful for forgiveness. After all, man, I'm a Christian!" And that's the trouble.

If you say, "Of course, I'm grateful for forgiveness," check your attitude. Maybe you're not very grateful. Maybe in your head you know you should be grateful, you know Jesus paid a big price, and you know you've been forgiven. So you say, "Yeah, I'm grateful." But is it an overwhelming gratitude to Jesus for what He did for you?

I have a feeling that there are too many people in church these days who are ungrateful for the incredible gift of God's forgiveness. Have you ever given a gift to someone for their birthday or Christmas, you worked really hard, saved up your money, purchased the gift, put a lot of thought into it, wrapped it, gave it to them, and they unwrapped it and said, "Oh, that's nice," as they quickly went on to the next present? Remember that horrible feeling you felt in your heart when they did that? They didn't realize the sacrifice you made or the thought and care you put into it. They just opened it and said, "That's really nice," with their lips but not their heart.

I wonder if that's how God feels many times about us. He has given us this incredible gift of forgiveness, paid for by the terrible price of the blood of His only Son, and we say, "Oh yeah, I'm grateful for forgiveness." God doesn't want our lip service. He wants our thankfulness to Him to come from the very depths of our heart.

Look deep inside yourself. Are you really grateful for what has happened in your life?

Write a brief description of eternity in hell.

Nothing is how you want it. No

loved ones, no fun, nothing

good

Now write a brief description of eternity in heaven.

Perfect, people you love, everything you love, just perfection.

Now praise God He made a way for you to be with Him in heaven!

CHECKLIST:

☑ Today, read Matthew 19.

☒ Is there any sin you need to repent of today?

☒ Are you grateful that God has forgiven you?

☒ Spend some time praising and worshipping God.

☒ Pray over your own life and your day today.

☒ Pray for your family, friends, and those in authority.

☒ Pray for the people of the world to be saved.

☐ Ask God if He wants you to go on a mission trip next summer.

Do You Have an Attitude of Gratitude?

Day 2

. . . .

An Example of Gratitude

Therefore, I tell you, her many sins have been forgiven — for she loved much. But he who has been forgiven little loves little.

Luke 7:47

In Luke 7:36-47, we read the story of a woman who had an encounter with Jesus. She was a known adulteress. She was embarrassed and ashamed of herself. Society looked down on her with contempt and disgust, like we would a modern-day prostitute. Many people would think this is one of the worst kinds of sin you could commit. Yet Jesus forgave her, restored her, and gave her total acceptance.

In verse 38 it tells us she began to weep uncontrollably, washing Jesus' feet with her tears and wiping them with her hair. What an incredible sign of gratitude! Here was a woman who was very grateful, because she knew what she had been forgiven of.

Do you know what you've been forgiven of? Most of us think, *Oh yeah. I'm grateful for forgiveness, and grateful that He forgave me of all my sins and stuff.* But we really don't think that our sin is that bad. We think, *I'm not a prostitute, I'm not a murderer, I'm not a bank robber, and I haven't raped anyone. I'm not a really bad sinner.* As a result we're not very grateful, because we don't think that we have committed really bad sins to begin with.

We think of Jesus on the cross and think, *Oh man, that was really sad that He went to the cross just for my little sin. I can understand that He had to go to the cross for someone who committed a lot of sins, but not for just a little sin like I've had. But yeah, I'm thankful.*

It's not how big or small the sin, but the separation from God it causes that we're talking about. The Bible says in Psalm 51:5 KJV that we were born in sin, we were conceived in iniquity. That means we were made out of this stuff, so whether we've killed someone or just lied, it doesn't matter. It's not so much what we do — it's the state of our heart. We are born into a state of sin, and it's that state of sin that caused Jesus to go to the cross — so He could change our heart. He didn't die to change the things we did, but to change what we are on the inside which would change the things we did.

When we realize that Jesus paid the ultimate price to change what we are on the inside, our heart ought to be overwhelmed with gratitude. He gave His life to change our heart, to change the person we were born as so we could be born again as a son or daughter of the Most High God. He laid down His life so we could have a new, fresh, clean, and redeemed heart.

The woman in this Scripture was grateful because she knew what she had been forgiven of. We need to take a good look at our life and realize the gravity of our condition. Before Jesus came into our heart, we were on our way to hell with a heart that was dark and deserving of eternal death, but Jesus paid the price to redeem us. We need to stop and realize that our small sin is just as great as her big sin, because it's not the things that we do that make us a sinner, it's the state of our heart. That's why Jesus gives life — to change the state of our hearts.

Chew on this today and let your heart be overwhelmed with gratitude towards the Lord for forgiveness.

But he was pierced for our transgressions, he was crushed for our iniquities; the punishment that brought us peace was upon him, and by his wounds we are healed.

Isaiah 53:5

How does this Scripture verse affect you?

_____

_____

_____

_____

_____

_____

_____

_____

CHECKLIST:
• • • • • • • • • • • • •

☒ Today, read Matthew 20.

☐ Is there any sin you need to repent of today?

☐ Are you grateful that God has forgiven you?

☒ Spend some time praising and worshipping God.

☐ Pray over your own life and your day today.

☒ Pray for your family, friends, and those in authority.

☐ Pray for the people of the world to be saved.

☐ Ask God if He wants you to go on a mission trip next summer.

Do You Have an Attitude of Gratitude?

Day 3
●●●●●●●●●●●●●●●●●●●●●

HE WHO HAS BEEN
FORGIVEN MUCH...

Then he turned toward the woman and said to Simon, "Do you see this woman? I came into your house. You did not give me any water for my feet, but she wet my feet with her tears and wiped them with her hair.

"You did not give me a kiss, but this woman, from the time I entered, has not stopped kissing my feet.

"You did not put oil on my head, but she has poured perfume on my feet.

"Therefore, I tell you, her many sins have been forgiven — for she loved much. But he who has been forgiven little loves little."

Luke 7:44-47

This was very profound. Jesus was commenting on the state of the woman's condition — the condition of *her* heart — versus the condition of *Simon's* heart. They were each well-meaning people, yet the expression of gratitude was different. She was overcome with gratitude and he showed no gratitude. From the moment Jesus walked into the Pharisee's home, this woman served Jesus the only way she knew how, yet none of the others did anything for Him. He even pointed that out to them.

Then Jesus said these words that shocked me, "He who has been forgiven much loves much, but he who has been forgiven little loves little." Think about that for a minute. This woman knew she had been forgiven of a lot of things, hence the passionate response of gratitude to Jesus. Yet when we don't completely understand all we've been forgiven of, we love little. That means everything is a burden to us. We think it is a hassle to serve Jesus, to love Him, and to be committed to Him. Christianity is a drudgery — everything we do seems to be drawn out, unimportant, and boring. As a result, we love little. Why? Because we think we've been forgiven little. The fact is, we've been forgiven a lot, but we just don't always realize it.

If we think we've been forgiven little, we love little. Churches are full of people who love Jesus a little bit. Are you grateful for forgiveness? If someone asks you to do something for the Lord, do you act like you're all put out and being very inconvenienced? Do you think, *How could you possibly ask such a thing?* This is characteristic of someone who loves little, because when you love someone a lot, you'll do anything for them.

Judge your heart. Do you love little? Do you express love for Jesus just a little bit without any passion, because maybe you think you've been forgiven a little? Are you really grateful for your forgiveness? Or do you not really understand the magnitude of the debt He's paid for you? If you find in your heart that the expression of your love is lukewarm, watered down, or an obligated kind of love, then maybe you're loving little because you think you've been forgiven little.

It's time now to realize the bigness of the amount of forgiveness He gave you — you have a new life! Think about that.

What you have done wrong in the past can stay in the past. You can look to tomorrow with hope. You have a promising future. God forgives you!

Last week you made a list of all the sins you needed to deal with. Take that list out and praise God that because Jesus spilled His blood, you are forgiven of every one of them.

I thank God I am forgiven of:

_____

_____

_____

_____

CHECKLIST:

☑ Today, read Matthew 21.

☒ Is there any sin you need to repent of today?

☑ Are you grateful that God has forgiven you?

☑ Spend some time praising and worshipping God.

☒ Pray over your own life and your day today.

☑ Pray for your family, friends, and those in authority.

☑ Pray for the people of the world to be saved.

☐ Ask God if He wants you to go on a mission trip next summer.

Do You Have an Attitude of Gratitude?

Day 4

WITH YOUR WHOLE HEART

By him therefore let us offer the sacrifice of praise to God continually, that is, the fruit of our lips giving thanks to his name.

Hebrews 13:15 KJV

One of the evidences that we love little is, when we go to church and people start singing, we just stand there and mouth the words. We sort of sing them in our head, but we're not singing them with our heart, because the words have no meaning to us. Real worship isn't just singing songs in church. Real worship is singing from our heart to the King, to the Lord Jesus Christ. The Bible says **the fruit of our lips giving thanks.** Are our lips telling the Lord we are thankful and grateful, that we are genuinely, passionately, and completely overwhelmed with gratitude for what He has done for us?

Different people worship in different ways — some people lift their hands, some bow down on their knees, and some sit down in their seats. It's not the *style* that matters. What matters is the condition of your *heart*. Whether you're singing songs off an overhead projector or reading them out of a hymnal, if you don't mean them from your heart and you're not singing them passionately to your God, you're showing that you love little. You're shallow. You're saying the words, but they're not coming from your heart.

When you realize how incredible Jesus is and the price He paid for your forgiveness, gratitude should overwhelm you. That's exactly what He wants. He wants to capture your heart in worship. He wants you to wrap both arms around Him and sing passionately to Him from the bottom of your heart — more passionately than you would ever sing a love song to a boyfriend or girlfriend, because this is the King of life. This is the One who breathed life into you and made your heart beat in a brand new way. He grabbed hold of every piece of your heart and you are so eternally grateful for the incredible price He paid, for all He has done, and for everything He has created by the words of His mouth, that you sing *passionately*.

If you haven't made passionate worship part of your everyday lifestyle, commit now that when you have your quiet times you will show the Lord how very grateful you are for the price He paid. Show Him that you do love much, because you're not just going through the motions in worship, but you are worshipping Him with *all* of your heart.

Don't just sing for the sake of singing, but sing with all of your heart. Get a worship tape and sing along with the songs. Don't let the CD or the cassette do the worshipping for you, but *you* sing. It will be an encouragement for you as you really focus on the Lord and worship every morning in your quiet time before you start your day.

You're getting tight with God, and you're expressing the gratitude overflowing your heart to Him by worshipping Him.

Today I sang the following songs of praise and worship to Jesus:

_____

_____

_____

_____

_____

_____

_____

CHECKLIST:
• • • • • • • • • • • • • •

- [x] Today, read Matthew 22.
- [x] Is there any sin you need to repent of today?
- [x] Are you grateful that God has forgiven you?
- [x] Spend some time praising and worshipping God.
- [x] Pray over your own life and your day today.
- [x] Pray for your family, friends, and those in authority.
- [x] Pray for the people of the world to be saved.
- [ ] Ask God if He wants you to go on a mission trip next summer.

DO YOU HAVE AN ATTITUDE OF GRATITUDE?

Day 5

PASSION FOR THE WORD AND PRAYER

Jesus said in Luke 7:47 that he who is forgiven much loves much. If you realize you've been forgiven much, then you will love much. So ask yourself, "Do I really love the Lord a lot?"

We all say, "Well, of course we do." But when you're reading His Word, are you hungry for it? Are you aggressively looking for what God is trying to teach you as you read? Or are you just saying, "Okay, I guess it's time to read the Bible."

In prayer, are you pouring out your heart and letting God hear the depth of your soul cry out, or are you just going through your prayer list? How you pray indicates the attitude of gratitude in your heart and your love for Him.

Think about how you feel towards your mom and dad when you're away on a trip for a long time. You can't wait to come home. You can't wait to see them and tell them all about the things you did while you were away. When I get home from work at the end of the day, I love it when my three small children crawl up in my lap and snuggle all around me. They can't wait to tell me what they did all day. That's the picture you ought to have in your mind of what should happen every morning when you get up to have your quiet time. You can't wait to have an intimate time with your heavenly Father, sharing the secrets of your heart with Him, preparing yourself for the day, and learning from the Word of God what He wants to speak to you before pouring out your heart to Him in prayer.

It's time to start loving Him much, because you realize you've been forgiven much. It's time to start loving Him by listening to His Word and by really connecting to Him every day in prayer. Let's start today.

What are the most pressing questions about the Bible or problems on your heart that you are facing today?

Is it really bad that I to work on Sundays? And make others work by eating out.

CHECKLIST:

☒ Today, read Matthew 23.

☒ Is there any sin you need to repent of today?

☒ Are you grateful that God has forgiven you?

☐ Spend some time praising and worshipping God.

☒ Pray over your own life and your day today.

☒ Pray for your family, friends, and those in authority.

☒ Pray for the people of the world to be saved.

☐ Ask God if He wants you to go on a mission trip next summer.

Look up verses in the Bible that relate to your situation. Take them to God in prayer and ask Him what to do. Put the problem in God's perspective and get focused on truth! You will never be the same, because when you know the truth, the truth sets you free.

Do You Have an Attitude of Gratitude?

Day 6

ARE YOU TIRED OF THE "STORY"?

We've talked these last several days about being grateful for your forgiveness, and we've talked about what Jesus did on the cross for you. I wonder if the thought has crossed your mind, *Oh yeah, Jesus died on the cross and all that stuff.*

Too many people are way too casual when they think about what Jesus did on the cross. Think about the pain He suffered in His physical body as He was being nailed to the cross. Think about Him bearing all of our sins so we could be made righteous and have a relationship with the living God. That sheds a whole new light on being grateful for our forgiveness, being grateful for what happened to Jesus on the cross, and being grateful for what He did for us on the cross.

If you've been in Sunday school or church your whole life, you've heard the crucifixion story so many times. You can recite the story and you can quote verses about it verbatim, yet for too many people it's just the "story."

People say, "Oh yeah, it's that Jesus-died-on-the-cross thing." That's what the world thinks. They think they know it all, but they don't know the power or the meaning behind the crucifixion and resurrection of Jesus Christ. I'm afraid that too many people who call themselves Christians don't even know the power or the meaning behind the "story." They know it had to happen in order for them to be saved, but they're not appreciative to the Lord for what He did. As Christians, no matter how mature, how strong, or how old we get in the Lord, we can never forget or get far away from that story, because it is the truth of that story that changed our lives. It is the power of that story that set us free. It is the reality of that story that gave us new hearts. It's not just a story — it's what happened to the Son of God. It's Jesus Christ choosing to lay down His life for us.

Jesus even gave us the Lord's supper. He told His disciples in Luke 22:19, **do this in remembrance of me.** In other words, He was telling them, "Remember Me and that I was really here. Remember that I really died. See this blood? Remember My blood, because it's the new covenant. See this bread? Remember how My body was broken for you. Don't ever forget this story, don't ever forget that I died to give you eternal life, and don't ever think of it as just another parable or another folklore tale. This is real. I am real. I came and I laid down My life."

Check your own heart. Has the "story" just become another story to you? Or are you overwhelmed with gratitude to God every time you think of what He really did. If it's just become the story of Jesus on the cross to you, I encourage you right now to pray this prayer.

Oh Lord, help me to understand the reality of what really happened on the cross. Help me to really see how the cross was the crossroads of all history. That time in history when Jesus hung on the cross is the moment I'm grateful for, for without it I would be nothing. I would have no hope of eternal life in heaven and I would have no hope of a good life here in this earth. In Jesus' name I pray, amen.

CHECKLIST:
• • • • • • • • • • • • •

- ☑ Today, read Matthew 24 and 25.

- ☒ Is there any sin you need to repent of today?

- ☒ Are you grateful that God has forgiven you?

- ☒ Spend some time praising and worshipping God.

- ☒ Pray over your own life and your day today.

- ☒ Pray for your family, friends, and those in authority.

- ☒ Pray for the people of the world to be saved.

- ☐ Ask God if He wants you to go on a mission trip next summer.

Do You Have an Attitude of Gratitude?

Day 7

REMEMBER THE MOMENT

We need to make sure we don't just have a mental Christianity, but rather a life-changing encounter with Jesus. Is He really real to you? Are you grateful for forgiveness? Do you remember the exact moment you felt the weight of sin lift off your shoulders?

I remember feeling it when I was sixteen years old. I remember sensing this overwhelming drudgery and burden on my back, and all of a sudden I realized I was clean, I was free, I was whole, I was forgiven, and I was new. The burden was gone, my heart was right, and I was a new person. It's hard to describe it with words, but I'll never forget the moment when I realized I was really forgiven, when I realized that the weight of sin had been lifted off my shoulders. That is what the woman felt as she wept at Jesus' feet, as she washed His feet with her tears and hair. She felt the weight leave her, and her natural response was deep gratitude to the Son of God who cleansed her. She had a revelation of who Jesus was. He really was the

Son of God. He really had forgiven her and she was moved with gratitude.

Do you remember that moment? Maybe you don't remember that moment, because you've never had that moment. Maybe you have always thought, *Yeah, I'm forgiven,* but there has never been a time that you stopped and said, "Lord, forgive me, cleanse me, and take the weight of sin right now."

If you've never had that moment, or maybe you have asked for forgiveness but you never sensed the weight being removed, I want you to pause right now and pray this prayer.

Lord, I refuse to go through my life without being grateful for forgiveness. Right now, Lord, I ask You to take the weight of sin off of my life. I ask You to quicken to my mind the bigness of my sin so I can be truly grateful for having it lifted off of me.

Jesus, I thank You for paying that ultimate price, for dying on the cross for me. I thank You for lifting me, cleansing me, washing me, and making me new. Let my heart be overwhelmed with gratitude, because You died for me. Jesus, You gave Your life for me. I don't know if I've got a friend who would give their life for me, but You gave Your life for me when I was born in sin. Thank You, Lord, for taking the weight of sin off my life. In Jesus' name I pray, amen.

Hopefully by now you are sure that Jesus is real and Christianity is not just a ritual to you. You're not filling your head with a bunch of useless doctrine, but you are living a life that's been changed.

Everyday, ask the Lord to reveal any sin in your life and make sure your first response is to get rid of it by asking the Lord to forgive you. Be like Zacchaeus.

And once you know you have been forgiven, commit to be grateful for the Lord's forgiveness. Be grateful that He has lifted such a weight off you. Be thankful for the washing, for the cleansing, and for the mercy He has on you. Be thankful for what Jesus did on the cross for you.

Tell how Jesus has changed your life in these first few weeks of your Spiritual Shock Treatment.

_____
_____
_____
_____
_____
_____
_____
_____

CHECKLIST:

☑ Today, read Matthew 26 and 27.

☑ Is there any sin you need to repent of today?

☒ Are you grateful that God has forgiven you?

☒ Spend some time praising and worshipping God.

☑ Pray over your own life and your day today.

☑ Pray for your family, friends, and those in authority.

☑ Pray for the people of the world to be saved.

☐ Ask God if He wants you to go on a mission trip next summer.

chapter 4
CAN SOMEONE TALK YOU OUT OF IT?

For the word of God is living and active.
Sharper than any double-edged sword, it penetrates
even to dividing soul and spirit, joints and marrow;
it judges the thoughts and attitudes of the heart.

Hebrews 4:12

Day 1

THE TRUTH OF THE BIBLE

I want you to dig down deep inside your heart and decide whether you're just mentally agreeing with the Bible, or whether Jesus is really real in your life. First of all, I hope you're asking yourself every day what your response to sin is. Are you ready to get rid of it immediately? Secondly, are you really grateful for what Jesus did for you on the cross? The third question I have for you is what we will talk about this week. Is it possible for anyone to talk you out of your Christianity? Are you logically trying to understand what the Bible has to say, or has the truth of the Bible come alive in you?

So many people understand the Bible, but they've never really committed their lives to it — they've never had a revelation deep in their hearts that the Bible is God's Word to *them*. They've been convinced by a preacher, by a band at a Christian concert, or by an emotional moment at camp that they should pray the salvation prayer and get close to God, but without understanding God's Word is real, they have no way to get close to Him.

If someone can persuade you to follow Jesus, then someone else can persuade you not to. That's why so many people get convinced at camp to give their lives to Jesus, then they go back to school and the peer pressure convinces them otherwise. They attend a revival and get convinced they should follow the Lord again, then they go to a movie and it convinces them not to follow the Lord. Then they go back to church and they're convinced they should live for Jesus, until they go to a party and are convinced not to. If someone can convince you to follow Jesus, then the world can talk you out of it.

CHECKLIST:

☑ Today, read Matthew 28.

☐ Is there any sin you need to repent of today?

☐ Are you grateful that God has forgiven you?

☒ Have you been talked out of any part of your Christianity?

☐ Spend some time praising and worshipping God.

☐ Pray over your own life and your day today.

☐ Pray for your family, friends, and those in authority.

☑ Pray for the people of the world to be saved.

☒ Ask God if He wants you to go on a mission trip next summer.

This is the essence of a cerebral Christian. They have all the logical reasons of why they should believe, so they believe. But if anything comes against those logical reasons, they're no longer convinced. They know in their head, but they haven't had an experience in their heart. The reality of Jesus hasn't changed their life. In their head they agree that everything that the Bible says is true, but the truth of the real person that Jesus is hasn't shocked them, stunned them, and caused their heart to come alive.

I'm going to ask some serious soul-searching questions this week and show you from the Bible that Jesus wants us to be more than just convinced — He wants us to be converted. We're to be so convinced that we commit our life to Him, which results in a change on the inside of us. Get ready to be changed.

Is your faith in God based on what you can understand with your mind? Or have you experienced the reality of Jesus and nothing can persuade you differently?

CAN SOMEONE TALK YOU OUT OF IT?

Day 2

AGAINST ALL LOGIC

On hearing his words, some of the people said, "Surely this man is the Prophet."

Others said, "He is the Christ." Still others asked, "How can the Christ come from Galilee?

"Does not the Scripture say that the Christ will come from David's family and from Bethlehem, the town where David lived?"

John 7:40-42

Jesus could have logically convinced people who He was, but He chose not to. When people argued that the Messiah wasn't supposed to come out of Nazareth, Jesus just sat there and listened to them. He did not respond. Now think about it. Jesus was the smartest person who ever lived. He knew the Scriptures and the prophecies better than anyone else. He could have taken those Scriptures and blown them away. He could have logically convinced them that He came out of Bethlehem, was born of a virgin, and was from the line of David. But He chose not to.

When we talk to someone about the Lord, we want to use all kinds of scriptures and reasons to make them believe logically that Jesus is real. But the fact is, Jesus is so much bigger than logic. The God who created this world is beyond our human ability to logically understand Him. Jesus could have convinced them logically, but in doing so He would have *belittled the bigness of the truth He had come to share with them.*

People can be logically convinced and still not change. In trying to tell someone about the Lord, you can logically have all your arguments lined up, but they still may not believe. You can even get them to contradict themselves, yet if their heart is hard and they have blinders on their eyes, they still won't believe.

Jesus knew that the truth He had come to share was so much bigger than logic that He blew right past the logic to get into men's hearts — to get them to see with the eyes of their hearts and not just with the logic of their minds. Too many people are "logical" Christians, or mental Christians. They believe in Jesus as long as it makes sense. But as soon as it defies their logic — boom, they're out because it doesn't compute in their head. They think their mind is all-knowing, and if they're unable to figure something out with their mind then it must not be real or true.

Jesus chose not to use logic to woo people's hearts, but did a number of other things to try to prick their hearts so their eyes would be opened, they would see the truth, and see Him for who He really is. Today, put aside the logic that says that if you can't figure it out in your head, it must not be true. Truth is knowing your life has been changed forever by the living God. Truth is knowing you have been forgiven of your sins. Truth is knowing Jesus is real in your life!

Are you a logical Christian? _____

_____

_____

can someone talk you out of it?
● ●
against all logic

_____

_____

Do you believe in Jesus as long as it makes sense?

_____

_____

_____

_____

Have you allowed the Lord to remove the blinders from your spiritual eyes so you can see truth?

CHECKLIST:
● ● ● ● ● ● ● ● ● ● ● ● ●

☐ Today, read Mark 1.

☐ Is there any sin you need to repent of today?

☐ Are you grateful that God has forgiven you?

☐ Have you been talked out of any part of your Christianity?

☐ Spend some time praising and worshipping God.

☐ Pray over your own life and your day today.

☐ Pray for your family, friends, and those in authority.

☐ Pray for the people of the world to be saved.

☐ Ask God if He wants you to go on a mission trip next summer.

Can Someone Talk You Out of It?

Day 3
....

DRAWN BY GOD

But as I told you, you have seen me and still you do not
believe.

All that the Father gives me will come to me, and whoever
comes to me I will never drive away.

No one can come to me unless the Father who sent me
draws him.

John 6:36,37,44

Jesus said that God the Father must draw people to Him. It
is God the Father who must open people's eyes. In other words,
the reality of Jesus is much bigger than the logic you understand
with your mind. You have to understand that Jesus is real with
your heart. I'm not going to try to convince anyone. I'm just
trying to provoke people to have faith so they can open their
eyes and see the truth that God's been wanting them to see for
a long time.

So many people try to live their life for God based only on
what they understand logically. They try to tell others about

Jesus by telling them, "If you just believe what I believe, then you'll be saved." That's not what this Bible verse says. Jesus is saying that you have to believe in Him so much that you commit your life to Him. If you're going to commit your whole heart and your whole life to Jesus, you had better open up your eyes and see this truth for how big and how awesome it is. The reality of Jesus and living for Him is so big and so awesome that it's going to demand *all* of your heart.

Jesus didn't want to logically convince people, He wanted God to convince people. He wanted them to allow the Holy Spirit to open their eyes and for them to be stunned with the reality that He really was the Son of God. As a result, they would never be the same again — they would come running to Him, fall on their knees, give their life to Him, and be different forever.

Ask the Father God to open your eyes so you can see Jesus for who He really is today. Be like Moses and ask Him to give you a glimpse of His glory. Then watch out, because He's going to draw you closer and closer to Him.

What is the Father God showing you today?

_____

_____

_____

_____

_____

_____

_____

CHECKLIST:
• • • • • • • • • • • • •

☒ Today, read Mark 2.

☒ Is there any sin you need to repent of today?

☐ Are you grateful that God has forgiven you?

☐ Have you been talked out of any part of your Christianity?

☐ Spend some time praising and worshipping God.

☐ Pray over your own life and your day today.

☐ Pray for your family, friends, and those in authority.

☐ Pray for the people of the world to be saved.

☐ Ask God if He wants you to go on a mission trip next summer.

Can Someone Talk You Out of It?

Day 4

JESUS TRIED TO TALK PEOPLE OUT OF IT

Jesus said to them, "I tell you the truth, unless you eat the flesh of the Son of Man and drink his blood, you have no life in you.

Whoever eats my flesh and drinks my blood has eternal life, and I will raise him up at the last day.

For my flesh is real food and my blood is real drink.

Whoever eats my flesh and drinks my blood remains in me, and I in him.

John 6:53-56

Think about this. Jesus gave a sermon that was really hard to understand. He talked about eating His flesh and drinking His blood, or they would have no part of Him. You may ask, "What do you mean, eat someone's human flesh and drink their blood?" That's what the Jews thought and they understandably got freaked out by it.

On hearing it, many of his disciples said, "This is a hard teaching. Who can accept it?"

He went on to say, "This is why I told you that no one can come to me unless the Father has enabled him."

From this time many of his disciples turned back and no longer followed him.

John 6:60,65,66

People said, "Well, you know what? I can't logically figure this out, so I'm outa here." The next thing Jesus did was issue an altar call. He asked the remaining disciples if they wanted to leave also. Jesus is the only guy I ever knew to give an altar call for people to leave and quit following Him! Just imagine, as the choir is singing you hear Jesus say, "Please, with no one looking around — I don't want to embarrass anyone — but if you don't want to follow Me anymore, please exit right now."

Essentially that's what Jesus was doing. He tried to talk people out of following Him, because He wanted to see who would just be the fans, who would just be in it for the good times, who just had it logically figured out, and whose eyes had really been opened to see that He was the Son of God.

There are going to be times in your walk with God when things just don't make sense. You won't understand everything, because He's God and you're a human being. You need to decide now how you're going to respond when things don't seem to make sense, because the world makes it look so logical to *not* follow God. It's in those moments that you have to know you are following Jesus because you know He is real, and there's nothing anyone can say or do that can change your mind.

People can try every logical argument, every scientific discovery, or anything that seems to make sense to the world to try to talk us out of serving Him, but with the faith we have in Jesus Christ that changed our life, we can look them right in the face and say, "You know what? You're right. Some of this doesn't make sense. But this one thing I know — Jesus has changed my life and I've never been the same. I remember feeling the weight of sin lift. I remember my heart being changed. I know He hears me and I know I hear Him. He is real. He's not just in my brain — He's in my heart and in my life. You can try to talk me out of it all you want, but I'm telling you — He's changed my life and I'll never be the same."

How are you going to respond if the world tries to talk you out of it?

_____

_____

_____

CHECKLIST:
• • • • • • • • • • • • •

☑ Today, read Mark 3.

☒ Is there any sin you need to repent of today?

☒ Are you grateful that God has forgiven you?

☒ Have you been talked out of any part of your Christianity?

☒ Spend some time praising and worshipping God.

☒ Pray over your own life and your day today.

☒ Pray for your family, friends, and those in authority.

☒ Pray for the people of the world to be saved.

☐ Ask God if He wants you to go on a mission trip next summer.

_____

_____

_____

_____

_____

_____

Let your faith in Christ rise up so you can boldly proclaim Who has changed your life.

CAN SOMEONE TALK YOU OUT OF IT?

Day 5
. . . .

WHERE ELSE COULD WE GO?

"You do not want to leave too, do you?" Jesus asked the Twelve.

Simon Peter answered him, "Lord, to whom shall we go? You have the words of eternal life.

"We believe and know that you are the Holy One of God."

John 6:67-69

The way the disciples responded when Jesus gave the invitation to leave is amazing. Their response gives us a glimpse of what was going on in their hearts. He asked them in the previous verses what it would take to prove He was the Son of God. Did they want to see Him go up to heaven and then come back down? Was that going to prove to them that He was real? Was that going to convince them to stay?

In other words, Jesus was saying, "If I do some huge and amazing miracle, will that convince you that I really am the Son of God? Go ahead and leave." Then when He asked His twelve disciples if they wanted to leave, their only response was to stay, because they knew He was the Holy One of God and they had nowhere else to go.

Now think about the power of that statement. It's simple, but it's true. Imagine Peter and John and the rest of the guys sitting around saying, "You know what, Lord? We don't understand that sermon either. It doesn't make any sense to us. In fact, it sounds pretty intense — eating flesh and drinking blood — and logically we can't figure it out. But we know and believe you are the Son of God. There is no one like You. You have changed our lives. Where could we go? We've discovered truth, and nothing else compares to the truth of knowing You. We can't logically explain all this, but we know that You're the Son of God and we can go nowhere else."

I can just imagine the sparkle in Jesus' eye after He heard them respond like that. The sparkle in His eye said, "Good, you guys have really got something, because in the face of all these other people turning away, you didn't turn away. In the face of not understanding everything you didn't back out."

Even Jesus Himself could not talk them out of following Him. I can just imagine the joy He felt, realizing they finally saw the truth. The fact is this, *if someone can talk you in to following Jesus, then someone else can talk you out of it.* But if God convinces you that He's real and that Jesus is His Son, then no one, not even Jesus Himself, can talk you out of following Him.

It's time to get convinced by God. Let Him open your eyes to see that Jesus really is the Son of God. When you discover that, you'll respond just like the disciples did, "Where else could I go and what else could I do? I know you're the Son of God. I've got to follow You."

Today ask yourself these questions:

If I wasn't following Jesus, what would I be doing?

_____

_____

_____

Who would I follow?

_____

_____

_____

Who would be my lord and my god?

_____

_____

_____

_____

_____

_____

_____

CHECKLIST:
· · · · · · · · · · · ·

☐ Today, read Mark 4.

☐ Is there any sin you
need to repent of today?

☐ Are you grateful that
God has forgiven you?

☐ Have you been talked
out of any part of your
Christianity?

☐ Spend some time
praising and worship-
ping God.

☐ Pray over your own life
and your day today.

☐ Pray for your family,
friends, and those in
authority.

☐ Pray for the people of
the world to be saved.

☐ Ask God if He wants
you to go on a mission
trip next summer.

CAN SOMEONE TALK YOU OUT OF IT?

Day 6

LET THE BLINDERS FALL

The god of this age has blinded the minds of unbelievers, so that they cannot see the light of the gospel of the glory of Christ, who is the image of God.

2 Corinthians 4:4

Men were blinded to the light of the Gospel back in Bible times and they are blinded now. When people's hearts and minds are blinded, they can't see Jesus for who He really is. Therefore, people try to explain it or try to logically figure it out, but they can't because Jesus speaks the language of the heart.

Maybe you have a hard time telling people about Jesus. You try to logically lay it all out there, when, really, Jesus is speaking the language of the heart. He's wanting to get into people's hearts, not just their minds. He wants you to fill your mind with His Word once you have Him in your heart, but first you have to get Him in your heart.

Jesus has chosen to bypass the mind, bypass logic, and get into people's hearts. Satan has blinded people's eyes so much that many times they will have amazing opportunities to see the work of God right in front of their face, yet they don't even recognize it. It is sad, but I believe that Satan has blinded the eyes of many people in today's churches who call themselves Christians. They go through the motions and they believe everything in their head, but their eyes are blinded to just how awesome and incredible Jesus is. They are saved because they don't want to go to hell, but they never enjoy a passionate, fervent relationship with the living God. In their mind they're convinced, but their life and their heart are not changed. Jesus gave His life to give us a converted, changed life on the inside. He paid the price to give us a new heart. Continue to ask God to open your eyes, so in no way are you blinded to the truth of the Gospel like many people in this world are.

In Matthew 16:17, when Jesus told Peter that flesh and blood did not reveal to him who He was, but rather His Father in heaven, it helped Peter to understand how he came to this realization. This wasn't something that Jesus had carefully explained to him. Jesus wasn't in Sunday school every day trying to convince Peter that He was the Son of God. This had been revealed to Peter by God the Father.

If you haven't gotten it yet, it's time to let God convince you. He wants to reveal Himself to you. He wants to remove the blinders from your spiritual eyes so you can get a glimpse of Jesus. And when you get a glimpse of Jesus and see Him for who He really is, you'll never be the same again.

Today, get honest and ask yourself:

Why am I a Christian?

_____

_____

_____

_____

_____

can someone talk you out of it?
● ●
let the blinders fall

Do I have a passionate, fervent relationship with Jesus?

_____

_____

_____

_____

_____

CHECKLIST:
● ● ● ● ● ● ● ● ● ● ● ● ● ●

☑ Today, read Mark 5 and 6.

☐ Is there any sin you
need to repent of today?

☐ Are you grateful that
God has forgiven you?

☐ Have you been talked
out of any part of your
Christianity?

☐ Spend some time
praising and worship-
ping God.

☐ Pray over your own life
and your day today.

☐ Pray for your family,
friends, and those in
authority.

☐ Pray for the people of
the world to be saved.

☐ Ask God if He wants
you to go on a mission
trip next summer.

CAN SOMEONE TALK YOU OUT OF IT?

Day 7
. . . .

FOLLOWING JESUS FOREVER

Jesus wanted Peter to understand that what he was saying was evidence that he had heard the voice of God, that he had gotten a glimpse of truth bigger than life itself. He wasn't logically convinced that Jesus was the Son of God, but God had opened his eyes to see the truth and he was convinced in his heart.

This is what being a Christian is all about. It's about following Jesus —the real Jesus — not some great leader who lived 2,000 years ago, but the Jesus who rose from the dead and is alive today. When you realize that in your heart of hearts, you're going beyond logic, beyond what all your friends say, beyond what peer pressure says, beyond what Hollywood says, beyond what rock-n-roll says, and beyond what rap music says. You're experiencing the reality of Jesus.

The world talks about God and there are many people who talk about Jesus, but in a very mental, cerebral kind of way. They say, "Oh yeah, Jesus saved me, Jesus this, and Jesus that." Even celebrities sometimes will say things about God or about Jesus.

But we're not talking about a Christianity that's comfortable or a Christianity that's convenient. We're talking about a heart that has been gripped by the reality of Jesus. A reality that drives you to your knees in prayer every day. A reality that causes you to wake up each morning and say, "Oh Jesus, how can I live for You today? I know You're real. I know You're alive and I must live for You with all my heart. No one talked me into it, so no one can talk me out of it."

When we ask ourselves the question, "Can someone talk me out of it?" we would all like to think, *Well, of course not.*

But I ask you these questions:

Has someone ever talked you out of *part* of your Christianity?

Has someone ever talked you out of boldly carrying your Bible to school?

Has someone ever talked you out of explaining your Christian T-shirt, or even wearing your Christian T-shirt?

If they can talk you out of *part* of your Christianity, they can talk you out of *all* of it. But when you have a revelation that Jesus is real, no one can ever talk you out of it again.

Make a list of reasons why you serve Jesus.

CHECKLIST:

- ☑ Today, read Mark 7 and 8.

- ☑ Is there any sin you need to repent of today?

- ☑ Are you grateful that God has forgiven you?

- ☑ Have you been talked out of any part of your Christianity?

- ☐ Spend some time praising and worshipping God.

- ☑ Pray over your own life and your day today.

- ☑ Pray for your family, friends, and those in authority.

- ☐ Pray for the people of the world to be saved.

- ☐ Ask God if He wants you to go on a mission trip next summer.

_____

_____

_____

_____

_____

_____

_____

chapter 5

STAYING STRONG

And we pray this in order that you may live
a life worthy of the Lord and may please him
in every way: bearing fruit in every good work,
growing in the knowledge of God, being strengthened
with all power according to his glorious might so
that you may have great endurance and patience.

Colossians 1:10, 11

Day 1
• •

IN SEARCH OF A MIRACLE

We always hear how big God is, so it would be easy to think that if God is big enough, He can convince all of us to give our hearts to Him — but that's not true. He doesn't *force* the gospel message on anyone. He can only draw people whose eyes and hearts are open and who want to know truth.

The Pharisees and Sadducees came to Jesus and tested him by asking him to show them a sign from heaven.

He replied, "When evening comes, you say, 'It will be fair weather, for the sky is red,'

"And in the morning, 'Today it will be stormy, for the sky is red and overcast.' You know how to interpret the appearance of the sky, but you cannot interpret the signs of the times.

"A wicked and adulterous generation looks for a miracu-lous sign, but none will be given it except the sign of Jonah."

Matthew 16:1-4

They were asking Him, "Come on — just show us a sign. If you show us a sign, then we can believe You're the Son of God." They were wanting Jesus to stoop to their level and show them a *logical*, tangible reason to believe He was the Son of God. He had been performing miracles all around them, but they didn't want to believe those — they wanted to see their own personal miracle.

Jesus wouldn't show the Pharisees and Sadducees a sign, because He knew the wickedness in their hearts. The only sign He was going to give them was the sign of Jonah, and they all knew the story about Jonah going into the city of Nineveh and warning the people of the destruction to come if they didn't repent from their evil ways. (See Jonah 1-3.) Jesus didn't want to convince them logically that He was the Son of God, because He didn't want their faith to be based on a miracle. He wanted their eyes to be opened and the truth to be revealed to them.

The problem is the attitude in their question. They were acting like they wanted to know Jesus only if He would show them a sign. That is how much of the world is. They will believe *if* they can see a sign. The very essence of that is a mocking atti-tude and spirit. In reality they were saying, "If You're so big and powerful, why don't You prove Yourself?"

Jesus was telling them, "With an attitude like that, you're not gonna get anything. Your eyes don't want to see. Your heart is not open to the things of God. You don't even want to know truth, so I'm not going to waste a miracle on that kind of attitude."

Many people today say, "Well, if God would just show me some kind of sign, then I would believe." But if their belief in Him is based on a miracle, what are they going to believe when the excitement of the miracle is gone? Will it take another, even more amazing miracle to hold their belief?

We've got to make sure we're not looking for another sign or another reason to believe in Jesus. We must base our faith and our life on knowing that Jesus is real. Our eyes have been opened and we can see Him for who He is. If we never see another miracle for the rest of our life, we know that Jesus is alive, because He's changed our life.

Is your belief in Jesus based on what He's done in your life or who He is?

_____

_____

_____

_____

_____

_____

_____

CHECKLIST:
• • • • • • • • • • • • • •

☒ Today, read Mark 9.

☒ Is there any sin you need to repent of today?

☒ Are you grateful that God has forgiven you?

☒ Have you been talked out of any part of your Christianity?

☒ Do you have a revelation of Jesus today?

☒ Spend some time praising and worshipping God.

☒ Pray over your own life and your day today.

☒ Pray for your family, friends, and those in authority.

☐ Pray for the people of the world to be saved.

☐ Ask God if He wants you to go on a mission trip next summer.

Staying Strong

Day 2

A Firm Foundation

This is why I speak to them in parables: "Though seeing, they do not see; though hearing, they do not hear or understand.

"In them is fulfilled the prophecy of Isaiah: 'You will be ever hearing but never understanding; you will be ever seeing but never perceiving.

"'For this people's heart has become calloused; they hardly hear with their ears, and they have closed their eyes.'"

Matthew 13:13-15

Many people say, "If I could just see a miracle, I'd believe," or "If You could show all my friends at school a miracle, then they would believe." But that's not true. This is what Jesus was addressing in Matthew. They saw the miracles and heard His preaching, yet they didn't believe.

Meanwhile a large crowd of Jews found out that Jesus was there and came, not only because of him but also to see Lazarus, whom he had raised from the dead.

So the chief priests made plans to kill Lazarus as well,

For on account of him many of the Jews were going over to Jesus and putting their faith in him.

John 12:9-11

When the Pharisees found out Jesus had raised Lazarus from the dead, instead of believing that Jesus was the Son of God, they said, "We've got to kill Jesus *and* Lazarus."

A miracle doesn't always settle the issue. Sometimes, as in the case of the Pharisees, it makes people more cynical. You would think it would make them stop and say, "Whoa, we are messing with the Son of God here." But no — raising Lazarus from the dead made them more mad and made them want to kill Jesus even more. If people's hearts do not want to know truth and their eyes aren't inclined to see truth, then no matter how many miracles happen in front of their face, they'll choose not to believe.

You can use miracles to try to get people to believe in Jesus. But people with hard hearts will often use those miracles to say that Jesus is the king of demons and that's why He casts out demons. They'll use those very same miracles to try to convince people that He's not the Son of God.

It's not a matter of logic, because even being convinced by miracles is not enough convincing. We can't base our faith in miracles. Our faith is in the God who does the miracles, because our eyes have been opened and we know that Jesus is the Son of God. When our faith is based on God and His Word, *nothing* can shake it.

The Bible says in the last days there will be false miracles from false prophets. (See Revelation 19:20.) If your faith is based solely on miracles from God, what's going to happen when the devil comes and we have false miracles? We've got to base our faith on the truth that Jesus is alive and we know He's changed our life, the truth that we see in the Word, and the truth in the fact that our eyes have been opened and we've gotten a glimpse of Him.

Therefore everyone who hears these words of mine and puts them into practice is like a wise man who built his house on the rock.

The rain came down, the streams rose, and the winds blew and beat against that house; yet it did not fall, because it had its foundation on the rock.

Matthew 7:24,25

What is your faith based on?

CHECKLIST:
• • • • • • • • • • • • • •

☐ Today, read Mark 10.

☐ Is there any sin you need to repent of today?

☐ Are you grateful that God has forgiven you?

☐ Have you been talked out of any part of your Christianity?

☐ Do you have a revelation of Jesus today?

☐ Spend some time praising and worshipping God.

☐ Pray over your own life and your day today.

☐ Pray for your family, friends, and those in authority.

☐ Pray for the people of the world to be saved.

☐ Ask God if He wants you to go on a mission trip next summer.

STAYING STRONG

Day 3

COME BACK FROM THE DEAD

There was a rich man who was dressed in purple and fine linen and lived in luxury every day.

At his gate was laid a beggar named Lazarus, covered with sores

And longing to eat what fell from the rich man's table. Even the dogs came and licked his sores.

The time came when the beggar died and the angels carried him to Abraham's side. The rich man also died and was buried.

In hell, where he was in torment, he looked up and saw Abraham far away, with Lazarus by his side.

So he called to him, "Father Abraham, have pity on me and send Lazarus to dip the tip of his finger in water and cool my tongue, because I am in agony in this fire."

But Abraham replied, "Son, remember that in your lifetime you received your good things, while Lazarus received bad things, but now he is comforted here and you are in agony.

"And besides all this, between us and you a great chasm has been fixed, so that those who want to go from here to you cannot, nor can anyone cross over from there to us."

He answered, "Then I beg you, father, send Lazarus to my father's house,

"For I have five brothers. Let him warn them, so that they will not also come to this place of torment."

Abraham replied, "They have Moses and the Prophets; let them listen to them."

"No, father Abraham," he said, "but if someone from the dead goes to them, they will repent."

He said to him, "If they do not listen to Moses and the Prophets, they will not be convinced even if someone rises from the dead."

Luke 16:19-31

This parable climaxes with the rich man asking Abraham to send Lazarus back from the dead so Lazarus could tell the rich man's brothers what happened to him. Then they would believe and wouldn't make the same mistake. Abraham's response was very profound.

Sadly, many think that if the miracle is big enough or if the sign is amazing enough, everyone will believe. But that's just not true. They knew the miracles God performed for Moses and the Prophets, but they didn't care about seeing the truth. Sending someone back from the dead was not going to convince them to believe in their hearts.

Again, Jesus doesn't logically convince people's minds — He goes after their hearts. Why? Because logically you can convince people that there is no God just as easily as you can convince them that there is a God.

For example, many times I have heard of someone who experienced a miracle healing and people excused it away by saying, "Oh yeah, well, they probably weren't really sick."

Doctors will say, "Well, they probably didn't have cancer after all. We must have misdiagnosed it."

Still others will say, "They probably recovered quickly because of all the vitamins they take."

People who are not inclined to truth will not be logically convinced anyway. They'll find ways to dismiss a miracle by thinking they were hallucinating or they weren't in their right mind.

This is another example that God doesn't use logical things to convince people. He wants to open people's eyes and convict their hearts, so when they commit their life and say they believe, they're doing it because they know Jesus is real.

Are you waiting for yet another miracle to *prove* something to you? Or are you able to believe God is real simply by what His Word says?

_____

_____

_____

_____

_____

_____

_____

Step out in faith and say, "God, I want to know You are real in my life. I don't want to look for signs and wonders only, but I want to put my trust and my faith completely in You."

CHECKLIST:

☐ Today, read Mark 11.

☐ Is there any sin you need to repent of today?

☐ Are you grateful that God has forgiven you?

☐ Have you been talked out of any part of your Christianity?

☐ Do you have a revelation of Jesus today?

☐ Spend some time praising and worshipping God.

☐ Pray over your own life and your day today.

☐ Pray for your family, friends, and those in authority.

☐ Pray for the people of the world to be saved.

☐ Ask God if He wants you to go on a mission trip next summer.

STAYING STRONG

Day 4
. . . .

PRAYING FOR MIRACLES

He said to Simon, "Put out into deep water, and let down the nets for a catch."

Simon answered, "Master, we've worked hard all night and haven't caught anything. But because you say so, I will let down the nets."

When they had done so, they caught such a large number of fish that their nets began to break.

So they signaled their partners in the other boat to come and help them, and they came and filled both boats so full that they began to sink.

When Simon Peter saw this, he fell at Jesus' knees and said, "Go away from me, Lord; I am a sinful man!"

Luke 5:4-8

There are times when people who are looking for truth will see miracles and it will confirm to them that Jesus is alive and real. In this passage of Scripture, the men had been out all night fishing, yet had caught nothing. Now keep in mind that this was their livelihood. They were fishermen by trade. Fishing is what put food on their tables and clothes on their backs. A night of fishing with nothing to show for it the next day was not a good thing. So it seemed a little ridiculous to go back out after cleaning their huge nets to try again — but they did simply because Jesus told them to. They were stepping out in faith.

When they ended up catching so many fish, Peter realized a miracle had taken place. They didn't just catch a few fish, they caught enough to fill up their boat and their friends' boat until they were on the verge of sinking. That's a lot of fish!

Something dawned on Simon Peter at that moment. He was looking for truth and answers and he had faith in his heart, so when the miracle happened in front of his eyes, it dawned on him that Jesus was the Son of God. He responded just like Zacchaeus and said, "Lord, depart from me for I'm a sinful man. I've got garbage in my life, and I don't even deserve to be around You."

The miracle helped Peter's spiritual eyes to be opened, because he already had faith in his heart. Does God still do miracles today? Absolutely! Should we pray for miracles? Absolutely! But miracles are not to *prove* who Jesus is to those who have no desire to have faith. He uses miracles to *provoke* their faith. Then their desire for truth and to know the living God explodes when they realize *this really is Him!*

Peter didn't focus in on the miracle, but rather he focused in on the One behind the miracle. The miracle is to point the way to the God behind the miracle. We're not to embrace the miracle, we are to embrace God.

When you realize that Jesus really is alive, He really does love you, and He really does want you to follow Him, your life will be changed forever. That reality removes the blinders from your eyes so you can see the truth.

Maybe you're saying, "I love Jesus with all my heart, but I really would like to see a miracle." I challenge you to take a look around you. There are miracles taking place all around that you probably aren't even aware of.

Are you breathing? That's the miracle of life! Can you say that everything you have or everything you have accomplished has been because of your own ability and your power? Of course not! Make a list of all the miracles in your life. I think you'll be surprised at how many turn up.

CHECKLIST:

☐ Today, read Mark 12.

☐ Is there any sin you need to repent of today?

☐ Are you grateful that God has forgiven you?

☐ Have you been talked out of any part of your Christianity?

☐ Do you have a revelation of Jesus today?

☐ Spend some time praising and worshipping God.

☐ Pray over your own life and your day today.

☐ Pray for your family, friends, and those in authority.

☐ Pray for the people of the world to be saved.

☐ Ask God if He wants you to go on a mission trip next summer.

STAYING STRONG

Day 5

FOR THOSE WHO HAVE EARS

Then Jesus said, "He who has ears to hear, let him hear."

Mark 4:9

Jesus often ended a parable with these words. It's almost as though Jesus was daring us to listen. It's as if He was saying, "You know, sometimes you hear Me, but you don't really listen. You see, but you don't really understand what you're seeing. It's more than just a story you're hearing — there's *truth* in this parable." It's almost like He was telling these parables and doing these miracles to provoke people's faith to see whose ears would perk up, to see who was hungry for truth, and to see whose eyes were opened.

Jesus would tell them, "Listen closely. If you really want this, you better listen tight." So those who wanted truth would come and listen again and again.

They would say, "Man, there's something real about this message. I can't quite figure it all out, but there's truth here.

There's something real about this guy. He speaks with authority and He talks like He's been there."

Jesus was challenging them, "Man, don't listen the way you normally do — listen with faith. Listen with an open heart."

He wanted to provoke those who would embrace Him once they discovered who He was. He does the same thing today. Jesus isn't going around and flexing His muscles saying, "I'm the Son of God. I'm the Son of God." He's looking for those with hungry hearts. He's looking for those who don't want to be convinced logically, but who want to be changed inwardly. He's looking for people who want an encounter with God every day — those who want to wrap their lives around Him.

Jesus is looking for people just like you to live that kind of life. He doesn't have to prove Himself — He knows who He is. He's looking for those who have eyes that want to be opened.

Do your eyes want to be opened?

God isn't going to make your heart hungry for truth — only you can make it happen. How? By making sure you have time with the Lord each and every day. After you read Mark 13 today, sing songs to Him and pray. Then write down what you saw when the Holy Spirit opened your eyes.

_____

_____

_____

This not only prepares you for the day, but you'll find yourself more and more hungry for the things of God tomorrow.

CHECKLIST:

☐ Today, read Mark 13.

☐ Is there any sin you need to repent of today?

☐ Are you grateful that God has forgiven you?

☐ Have you been talked out of any part of your Christianity?

☐ Do you have a revelation of Jesus today?

☐ Spend some time praising and worshipping God.

☐ Pray over your own life and your day today.

☐ Pray for your family, friends, and those in authority.

☐ Pray for the people of the world to be saved.

☐ Ask God if He wants you to go on a mission trip next summer.

STAYING STRONG

Day 6

CAN THE WORLD SEE JESUS IN YOU?

Now Thomas (called Didymus), one of the Twelve, was not with the disciples when Jesus came.

So the other disciples told him, "We have seen the Lord!" But he said to them, "Unless I see the nail marks in his hands and put my finger where the nails were, and put my hand into his side, I will not believe it."

A week later his disciples were in the house again, and Thomas was with them. Though the doors were locked, Jesus came and stood among them and said, "Peace be with you!"

Then he said to Thomas, "Put your finger here; see my hands. Reach out your hand and put it into my side. Stop doubting and believe."

Thomas said to him, "My Lord and my God!"

Then Jesus told him, "Because you have seen me, you have believed; blessed are those who have not seen and yet have believed."

John 20:24:29

In other words, Jesus was saying, "Blessed are those who know I'm real, even though they never personally touch my side."

If this is your attitude, then no matter what anyone says or does to you, they'll never convince you that Jesus isn't real because you *know* Him.

There's a story of two men who were in a Nazi concentration camp during World War II. One was a Christian minister and the other was a very smart intellectual atheist. The atheist kept mocking the Christian for his faith, "How can you believe in the Son of God? How do you know He's real? Have you ever seen Him?"

The minister responded one day, "Yes, I have seen Him."

"Oh really? I suppose you talk to Him too."

"Oh yes, I talk to Him."

Finally the atheist asked, "What does He actually look like?"

"Well," the minister said, "sometimes He smiles at me."

The atheist replied, "Oh really? He smiles at you? And what does He look like when He smiles?"

The minister, with a beaten, tattered old face from being in the prison camp for a number of years, looked up at this unbelieving atheist and began to smile with a glow from heaven.

This caused the atheist to totally change his heart and he responded by saying "Sir, I believe you have seen Jesus."

What is the world saying about you? Do your friends know you are a Christian because you tell them, or because you live it?

_____

_____

_____

_____

_____

If Jesus really has changed you on the inside, let it show on the outside. What changed this atheist's heart was not something he heard, it was something he saw. Let your words and your actions be the evidence of a Jesus-filled heart and a Jesus-changed life.

CHECKLIST:

☐ Today, read Mark 14 and 15.

☐ Is there any sin you need to repent of today?

☐ Are you grateful that God has forgiven you?

☐ Have you been talked out of any part of your Christianity?

☐ Do you have a revelation of Jesus today?

☐ Spend some time praising and worshipping God.

☐ Pray over your own life and your day today.

☐ Pray for your family, friends, and those in authority.

☐ Pray for the people of the world to be saved.

☐ Ask God if He wants you to go on a mission trip next summer.

STAYING STRONG

Day 7

WHAT EVIDENCE DO YOU GIVE?

We can logically talk about Jesus all we want, but as we've learned these past few weeks, Jesus never tried to logically convince anyone. The most important piece of evidence you have that shows people Jesus is real is *your life*. Your evidence is your life. If they can't see Jesus is real by the way you look at them, the way you talk to them, and the way you act, then you shouldn't try to convince them logically.

People will be convinced that Jesus is real when they *see* that a miracle has happened inside your heart and there's no way to explain it, except it must be God. Your friends need to see something much bigger than logic. They need to see that the power of the living God has shocked you and changed you. You might be human, but there's someone bigger than human who lives inside of you who is real and is blazing with love and compassion for people — ready to serve, to give, and to care. They need to see that there's a force outside of this world that has come to live inside of you — the very presence and love of Jesus Christ.

Am I convinced or am I converted?

Has Jesus really changed my life or is it just in my head?

Can someone talk me out of it?

Do I have a revelation of Jesus?

Ask yourself these questions each day. Then get on your knees and from the bottom of your heart cry out to God, asking Him to open up your spiritual eyes to get a glimpse of Jesus like you've never seen Him before. Let 2 Corinthians 5:17 come alive in your heart. Accept the fact that the old things in your life have passed away, all things have become new, and Jesus has changed you on the inside.

You're not perfect, but that is something you can strive for each and every day. Pray this prayer with me.

Lord, there are a lot of specific areas that I need to have changed, but I know You've changed me from darkness to light. I was dead on the inside, but now I am alive on the inside. Jesus, I need a glimpse of You. I want the evidence of a changed life to show this world. I don't want to just tell this world about You, but I want to show them by the way I live, by the way I love, and by the way I act, that I have met the Almighty God and His Son, Jesus Christ. In Jesus' name I pray, amen.

I encourage you to keep a pure heart. Check the sincerity of your heart on a regular basis. Have a pure, holy, and sincere desire to get more of God. Learn more about God and grow in Him, and that will keep you seeing Jesus in a very real way.

Your relationship with Jesus will never get stale or stagnant if you keep Jesus in front of your face and in your heart. If you will hold on to a pure heart, cleansed and forgiven by the blood of Jesus, you'll always see God.

1. Make a list of the things you do that portray Jesus.

    _____

    _____

staying strong

what evidence do you give?

_____

_____

_____

2.   Make a list of the things you do that don't portray Jesus.

_____

_____

CHECKLIST:

☐ Today, read Mark 16 and Luke 1.

☐ Is there any sin you need to repent of today?

☐ Are you grateful that God has forgiven you?

☐ Have you been talked out of any part of your Christianity?

☐ Do you have a revelation of Jesus today?

☐ Spend some time praising and worshipping God.

☐ Pray over your own life and your day today.

☐ Pray for your family, friends, and those in authority.

☐ Pray for the people of the world to be saved.

☐ Ask God if He wants you to go on a mission trip next summer.

_____

_____

_____

_____

_____

3.   Work on increasing the first list and diminishing the second list!

104

chapter 6

HAVE YOU GIVEN EVERYTHING TO JESUS?

*The kingdom of heaven is like
treasure hidden in a field. When a man
found it, he hid it again, and then in his joy
went and sold all he had and bought that field.*

*Again, the kingdom of heaven is like
a merchant looking for fine pearls.*

*When he found one of great value, he went away
and sold everything he had and bought it.*

Matthew 13:44-46

Day 1
. . . .

ARE YOU MOTIVATED
BY A SENSE OF OBLIGATION?

When we realize what Jesus has done for us, we ought to be willing to do anything in response. He left heaven, came to this earth as a human, suffered persecution, and was nailed to the cross just so we could have a relationship with God. Our hearts should be overwhelmed with so much gratitude that we are willing to do *anything* for Him. We can't do anything out of a sense of obligation to earn our salvation, because He paid the ultimate price.

So many people who have a cerebral kind of Christianity act like they're doing God a favor if they go to church on

Sundays. If they go on Wednesday night, they think they're practically a missionary!

There are many people who will stand out in subfreezing temperatures for hours — ignoring the sleet and snow— to get tickets to a ball game. They'll cheer, scream, and go crazy at this ball game they paid hundreds of dollars for, because they are that committed to their team. Yet, if it starts to rain a little bit on a Sunday morning, they won't go to church.

Is Jesus just in your head or has He really changed your life? You can answer that question with another question: How much am I willing to do for Jesus? When the pastor or the youth pastor asks for a volunteer, are you the first to volunteer, or do you say, "Oh man, do I gotta do that again?"

Have you thought about going on a mission trip — going somewhere to change the world? Or is your response, "Why do I have to do that? Do I have to do that to be a good Christian?" Is there a sense of *obligation* or is there a sense of *privilege?* Your response should be, "Wow, the Lord would let me do that? He would allow me to do something in His service to represent Him?"

What are you willing to do for Jesus?

_____

_____

_____

If you're not willing to do much, then I ask another question: Has He really changed your life? Is He just in your brain or has He really affected your heart and your life? If He has affected your heart and your life, you'll do anything for Him.

CHECKLIST:

☐ Today, read Luke 2.

☐ Is there any sin you need to repent of today?

☐ Are you grateful that God has forgiven you?

☐ Have you been talked out of any part of your Christianity?

☐ Will you give your all to Jesus today?

☐ Spend some time praising and worshipping God.

☐ Pray over your own life and your day today.

☐ Pray for your family, friends, and those in authority.

☐ Pray for the people of the world to be saved.

☐ Ask God if He wants you to go on a mission trip next summer.

HAVE YOU GIVEN EVERYTHING TO JESUS?

Day 2
MOTIVATED BY JOY

For where your treasure is, there your heart will be also.

Luke 12:34

Matthew 13:44-46 tells us the story of the man who discovered treasure in a field. He was so sure of the treasure that he sold everything to buy that field. That field was worth everything he had, because the treasure was there. He gave everything in exchange for the treasure. It meant that everything he owned, he no longer owned. This is a perfect picture of the kind of discovery Jesus wants us to make in Him.

Have you discovered the treasure of Jesus? Many times people feel like Christianity is an obligation, "Okay, I've got to go to church every week. I've got to wear these clothes. I can't do this, and I can't do that." It sounds like a bunch of rules obeyed out of obligation, but that's only if it's just in your head. If you're just a mental Christian, Christianity is a list of rules. But the man who found the treasure was so excited about what he found that he didn't care about selling all his stuff. **In his joy [he] went and sold all he had** (Matthew 13:44).

That's the kind of attitude that Christians who have been changed by the power of God carry with them. In their joy they give their life away. In their joy they give every piece of their heart to God. It's not a bunch of rules they now follow. They've had their life and their heart changed, and nothing really matters anymore. They realize what they had without Jesus Christ was nothing anyway, so they *joyfully* gave it up.

Are you serving Jesus out of a sense of obligation?

Are you a Christian just because you're supposed to be?

Do you consider it a privilege to give everything away so you can get this treasure?

Do you worship Jesus out of joy?

Do you follow Scripture out of joy?

Do you go to church, read your Bible, and have your quiet time out of joy?

You have made known to me the path of life; you will fill me with joy in your presence, with eternal pleasures at your right hand.

Psalm 16:11

But the fruit of the Spirit is love, joy, peace, patience, kindness, goodness, faithfulness,

Gentleness and self-control. Against such things there is no law.

Galatians 5:22,23

He gave you joy when you asked Him into your heart. Now it is up to you to exercise it. In everything you do, choose to respond with joy!

Make a list of situations where you need to improve in responding in joy:

_____

_____

_____

_____

_____

_____

CHECKLIST:
• • • • • • • • • • • • • • •

☐ Today, read Luke 3.

☐ Is there any sin you need to repent of today?

☐ Are you grateful that God has forgiven you?

☐ Have you been talked out of any part of your Christianity?

☐ Will you give your all to Jesus today?

☐ Spend some time praising and worshipping God.

☐ Pray over your own life and your day today.

☐ Pray for your family, friends, and those in authority.

☐ Pray for the people of the world to be saved.

☐ Ask God if He wants you to go on a mission trip next summer.

HAVE YOU GIVEN EVERYTHING TO JESUS?

Day 3

. . . .

DID YOU REALLY FIND THE TREASURE?

People who don't have joy in their Christianity have a serious question to ask. Did they really find the treasure? When the man in Matthew 13 found the treasure, he went hog-wild berserk and sold everything.

I can imagine his friends saying, "You're crazy! What are you doing that for?" Maybe that is what your friends said when you first gave your life to Jesus. If they did, that's okay. That means the change Jesus made on the inside of you was seen in your words and your actions. You were a changed person on the inside and the outside.

If they didn't think you had gone crazy, maybe they should have. Maybe they couldn't see any changes in your behavior. Maybe you didn't give every part of your life to Him. Maybe you're still hanging on to certain areas that you need to give to Jesus so He can completely cleanse you and set you free.

This man had to sell everything he had to buy the field where the treasure was. You may have to get rid of some things you're holding on to so you can get the treasure. You may need to get rid of some CD's, books, and magazines that are really just garbage in your life. You may need to stop watching certain types of movies. Realize that the treasure you have is more important than anything else.

Have you found the treasure?

Did you just go through the motions out of a sense of obligation?

Have you realized the awesomeness of knowing Jesus?

Check your own heart. When you discover the treasure, nothing else really matters. You're so mesmerized, excited, thrilled, turned on, stoked, and fired up about the treasure that you don't even care about what you have to give up to get it.

Have you really found the treasure?

_____

_____

_____

_____

_____

_____

_____

_____

_____

_____

CHECKLIST:
• • • • • • • • • • • • • •

☐ Today, read Luke 4.

☐ Is there any sin you need to repent of today?

☐ Are you grateful that God has forgiven you?

☐ Have you been talked out of any part of your Christianity?

☐ Will you give your all to Jesus today?

☐ Spend some time praising and worshipping God.

☐ Pray over your own life and your day today.

☐ Pray for your family, friends, and those in authority.

☐ Pray for the people of the world to be saved.

☐ Ask God if He wants you to go on a mission trip next summer.

HAVE YOU GIVEN EVERYTHING TO JESUS?

Day 4
• •

THE PEARL OF GREAT PRICE

Matthew 13:45 tells us another parable about finding a great treasure — a pearl of great price. When the merchant found the pearl, he also sold everything he had to buy this pearl. When you discover the pearl is worth more than anything else you've ever thought about having, then you gladly give up the things you thought were valuable.

Jesus is trying to reiterate the magnificence and the joy of knowing Him. He is the pearl. He is the treasure. It's a discovery we make — not something we're logically convinced of. When you discover the pearl and find the treasure, all of a sudden you find something worth more than everything else you have put together and you're willing to give it all up, because you found something that's totally amazing.

What does it mean to *sell all*? The man in the first story sold everything to buy the land so he could get the treasure. What does it mean for us as Christians to sell everything? We are used to hearing altar calls, "Just turn and give your life to Jesus. All you have to do is pray this prayer…," but Jesus never said, "All you have to do." He said He wants *everything.* He doesn't want *part* of our life, He wants *all* of our life.

We've got too many "all you have to do" kind of Christians. They want you to pray a prayer with them real fast, give your heart to Jesus, and everything will be fine — you can go on and live your life. But Jesus never said that. He compared it to this man. He said we must sell *all,* to give every part of our life to Him — even the ugly part.

When all was said and done, the only thing this man had was the treasure — which was worth far above anything he had to sell. It's the same with us. When we submit totally to Jesus, we are left with a great treasure — which is more valuable than anything we have to give up. That includes our private life, our free time, our summers, our time at school — we don't even own ourself anymore. He owns us. We belong to Him. He's our Lord and our boss. He's in charge.

When you sell everything to buy the field, it means you no longer own anything. When you give your life completely to Jesus, you don't own any part of it. Many Christians find the treasure, but they don't want to sell everything. They want to hang on to a few things and still have the treasure. So they think they have the treasure, but they don't because they haven't really sold out to God. They say, "Well, I have Jesus, but I'm going to hang on to some parts of my life, a few areas of my heart, and these pet habits." But they have nothing more than a taste of the treasure.

Have you found that pearl yet?

Are you listening to music that does not edify your spirit and bring honor to Jesus?

Are you spending too much time watching television and not enough time reading your Bible and praying?

Do your friends influence you in a worldly way or in a godly way?

Have you gotten rid of the things in your life preventing you from having the treasure within you? If you haven't, it's time to find the pearl of Jesus. Take inventory of the things that are important in your life. You can start with this list:

IMPORTANT THING	ACTION NEEDED TO PUT JESUS FIRST

CHECKLIST:

☐ Today, read Luke 5.

☐ Is there any sin you need to repent of today?

☐ Are you grateful that God has forgiven you?

☐ Have you been talked out of any part of your Christianity?

☐ Will you give your all to Jesus today?

☐ Spend some time praising and worshipping God.

☐ Pray over your own life and your day today.

☐ Pray for your family, friends, and those in authority.

☐ Pray for the people of the world to be saved.

☐ Ask God if He wants you to go on a mission trip next summer.

Make Jesus your treasure. Purpose today to put Him first in your life — far above anything else.

HAVE YOU GIVEN EVERYTHING TO JESUS?

Day 6

SHOWING PEOPLE THE TREASURE

Evangelism is nothing more than showing people the treasure of Jesus Christ. We don't have to convince them. We just have to do whatever we can to show them that Jesus really is the treasure. We don't have to logically try to get them to figure it all out, woo them, suck them in, or shove it down their throat to show them what an incredible treasure He is. He's the One they've been looking for. He's the One we're selling everything for. He's the One worth giving our hearts to and worth giving our lives for.

It's all about the treasure — it's all about Jesus. It's not about us, it's not about this scripture and that scripture and logically figuring it out, but He's the Son of God. He's the author of life. He's the giver of life. He's the changer of hearts. He's the treasure — the One who forgives, restores, and puts lives back together. He's the One we serve, the One who gave His life for us, and the One who paid the ultimate sacrifice for our eternal freedom and peace.

We just have to show people the treasure! They don't have to understand everything about the Bible or the Gospel. All they have to understand is that He's the answer to their question. He's the answer to their problem. He's the treasure worth giving their whole life for, so when we ask them to pray the salvation prayer, they're not just chanting a prayer with their brain. Their eyes have been opened and they can see that He's the treasure. They're ready to sell everything to buy that field, because they found the treasure that's in the field. As a result, they are prepared to sell out. They are prepared to relinquish ownership of their life in exchange for a relationship with Jesus.

Are you showing people the treasure of Jesus that is inside of you?

Knowing you have the treasure, are you looking to *Him* for the answers you need? Make a list of who you seek out when different situations occur in your life. Then ask yourself if you should go to Jesus first.

CHECKLIST:

☐ Today, read Luke 6 and 7.

☐ Is there any sin you need to repent of today?

☐ Are you grateful that God has forgiven you?

☐ Have you been talked out of any part of your Christianity?

☐ Will you give your all to Jesus today?

☐ Spend some time praising and worshipping God.

☐ Pray over your own life and your day today.

☐ Pray for your family, friends, and those in authority.

☐ Pray for the people of the world to be saved.

☐ Ask God if He wants you to go on a mission trip next summer.

SITUATION	PERSON I GO TO	JESUS FIRST?

HAVE YOU GIVEN EVERYTHING TO JESUS?

Day 7

GIVING HIM ALL

What are you willing to do for Him?

Are you willing to sell out?

If you've sold your whole field to buy the treasure, and if you've given your whole life in exchange for the life He gives you, then you'll do *anything* for Him. You don't care what it is. If He asks you to go to Africa or Asia on a mission trip, you'll go. If He asks you to quit cussing or quit smoking, you'll do it. None of that really matters, because He's given you *life.*

You may think, *Well, I don't know that the Lord has asked me to do anything specifically.* But what about your integrity and your character? Do you often ask yourself, "What would Jesus do or say in this particular situation?" Or do you make decisions based on what your friends think is cool?

Vindicate me, O Lord, for I have walked in my integrity; I have [expectantly] trusted in, leaned on, and relied on the Lord without wavering and I shall not slide.

Psalm 26:1 AMP

The righteous man is rescued from trouble, and it comes on the wicked instead.

Proverbs 11:8

What about being submissive to your mom and dad? Are you so set in your mind as to what you want to do that you don't even listen to anything your parents tell you? Just because you are a teenager doesn't mean you have to be rebellious. That is a lie from the pit of hell! How can you expect to hear from God, whom you can't see, when you don't listen to your parents, whom you can see? How can God trust you with a position of authority if you don't submit to and respect those who have been placed in authority over you?

Children, obey your parents in the Lord, for this is right.
"Honor your father and mother" — which is the first commandment with a promise —
"That it may go well with you and that you may enjoy long life on the earth."

Ephesians 6:1-3

Nothing on this earth can be compared to the greatness of the eternal life that's inside of you. If you haven't given all that you are in exchange for Jesus, the treasure, right now's the time to do it.

I want you to pray the following prayer with me. If you've already done this, then do it again. Make sure you've given everything to Him.

Lord Jesus, I give You my all. Every piece of my heart, every piece of my life, it all belongs to You. It doesn't belong to me. I give everything in exchange for the new life You give me, because I know You gave everything for me. I commit every part of me to You. It all belongs to You — my summers, my days at school, my time with my parents, my future, my career, my job, my college education, everything belongs to You. I submit my life to You, because You've given Your life and put it inside of me. In Jesus' name I pray, amen.

Ask Jesus today if there is something He would have you give up to have a closer relationship with Him. What did He say?

_____

_____

_____

_____

_____

_____

_____

_____

_____

_____

_____

_____

_____

_____

Be open to hear His voice. Be open to follow Him. Be open to the changes that are coming your way.

CHECKLIST:
• • • • • • • • • • • • • •

☐ Today, read Luke 8 and 9.

☐ Is there any sin you need to repent of today?

☐ Are you grateful that God has forgiven you?

☐ Have you been talked out of any part of your Christianity?

☐ Will you give your all to Jesus today?

☐ Spend some time praising and worshipping God.

☐ Pray over your own life and your day today.

☐ Pray for your family, friends, and those in authority.

☐ Pray for the people of the world to be saved.

☐ Ask God if He wants you to go on a mission trip next summer.

Conclusion to Part One

Congratulations for allowing the Holy Spirit to totally change you from the inside out! No longer are you a cerebral, mental Christian. You have been converted!

Up to this point I've given you status-quo Christianity. This is what normal Christianity should be about. It's the beginning of seeing eye-to-eye with Jesus. It's a heart-to-heart connection that pushes you to be real with Him every day.

You know that you and Jesus are connected. You have something real with Him. It's not just something mental in your brain, but it's a relationship and a bond with the living God that grips your heart and changes your life.

Daily you have examined different parts of your life. Now there's something fresh, new, and alive within you. Continue to check your heart to make sure there's no traditionalism, no mundane, petrified Christianity taking root inside of you.

Now that you have a concrete way of making sure you and Jesus have something real happening every day, it's time to go ballistic. It's time to go for broke. It's time to live on the edge — to push yourself out of your comfort zone. It's time to go off the deep end for God. It's time to grab every piece of the gusto that God ever wanted for you!

PART TWO

Go For Broke

Up to this point we've been talking about keeping your relationship with Jesus real. Now it's time to step off the ledge. It's time to get out of your "safety zone," or the zone that looks like it's good and acceptable Christianity. In the second part of this book we're going to talk about having the **edge** in your Christian life.

What is the edge?

What is the biting edge of the reality of Jesus?

How do you keep your edge sharpened so you don't become a dull, monotonous, traditional Christian?

Yes, you have your life with God right. But how do you keep your edge sharp so you are profound in all that you say and do? How do you make sure you never blend in? The realness of Jesus in your life demands that you make a difference wherever you are. Set the pace for your own generation — keep your spiritual edge sharp.

•

chapter 7
HAVING THE EDGE

Be joyful always;

Pray continually;

Give thanks in all circumstances,
for this is God's will for you in Christ Jesus.

1 Thessalonians 5:16-18

Day 1

WHAT IS THE EDGE?

Have you ever looked in someone's eyes and you could tell they just came out of the throne room of God. Then you wondered, *Why am I not like that?* They have the edge. They are a powerful Christian and you're not. You know Jesus, but you're not powerful. You don't have the edge.

There are a lot of people who go through the motions of Christianity, but they don't have the edge. Many in the ministry do what their job description says, or they do what they learned at a conference somewhere, but they don't have the edge.

Have you ever been so blessed by someone's preaching, you just wanted to jump up on your seat and scream, "AMEN! YEAH!"? Have you ever felt like that before? It's because that person ministering had the edge.

What's the edge?

The edge is the presence of the living God operating through you to change lives.

When you walk into your classroom or your school building, what are your friends and acquaintances thinking about you? Do they even know something is different about you? When you have the edge you may suffer persecution, but when a friend finds themselves in trouble, you're the first person they'll go to. They know you have an answer to their problem. They know you will point them in the right direction. They know you have what it takes to change their life.

When you have the edge, your prayers are powerful! When someone needs prayer, they come running to you. When you pray for lives to be changed — they are! When you pray for people to be healed — they are! Is it because of you? No! It is because the living God dwells BIG inside of you and that gives you the edge.

Someone who has the edge pushes past what is acceptable to what is powerful.

What was pretty good before is no longer good enough if you want the edge. You don't settle for second best, because you know God has only the best for you.

When you have the edge, you don't spend five minutes in prayer each week, feeling good about yourself because you fulfilled some "duty." No! You spend as much time as it takes to know you have been in the presence of the Almighty God and you have received the answers to your prayers.

When you have the edge, your time of praise and worship at home and in church is anointed because your entire being is focused totally on God. Your attitude throughout the day is one of worship, because you have such a heart of gratitude for all He's done for you.

Do you have a desire to see lives drastically changed?

Are you satisfied with your relationship with Jesus?

Are you willing to do whatever it takes to get the edge and keep it?

CHECKLIST:
· · · · · · · · · · · · · ·

☐ Today, read Luke 10.

☐ Is there any sin you need to repent of today?

☐ Are you grateful that God has forgiven you?

☐ Have you been talked out of any part of your Christianity?

☐ Will you give your all to Jesus today?

☐ Spend some time praising and worshipping God.

☐ Pray over your own life and your day today.

☐ Pray for your family, friends, and those in authority.

☐ Pray for the people of the world to be saved.

☐ Ask God if He wants you to go on a mission trip next summer.

☐ Do you have the edge to meet the challenges of your day?

HAVING THE EDGE

Day 2

HOW DO YOU GET THE EDGE?

God wants you to have the edge, but if you want it, you are gonna have to go for broke in the things of God! He wants you to have supernatural power and authority to use for His glory. But there are some things you'll have to do.

First of all, you need to examine your heart. Has God convicted you about something that you're not doing anything about? Do you do things that are contrary to your convictions? Suppose your friends want you to see a movie that you know contains a lot of cussing and sex. As a believer, you are careful about what you put into your mind, but your friends are really pressuring you into going with them. Are you going to heed the convictions of the Holy Spirit, or go along with the crowd to be accepted?

Secondly, you need to keep a heart of repentance. Get rid of secret sins. Live your convictions. Cut things off that don't belong there. You have been made the righteousness of Christ.

It is because of him that you are in Christ Jesus, who has become for us wisdom from God — that is, our righteousness, holiness and redemption.

1 Corinthians 1:30

Awake to righteousness, and sin not.

1 Corinthians 15:34 KJV

Thirdly, do more than what is expected of you in the Lord. You may say, "Well, I pray and read my Bible every day." Good. But if you want the edge, you have to do more than what everyone else is doing and more than what's expected.

Remember the parable of the rich *young* ruler in Luke 18:18-25? He asked Jesus, "What do I need to do to get to heaven?"

Jesus replied, "Well, you have to keep the commandments."

"But I've done all those since I was a little boy and I still don't have any life."

Jesus said, "Because you have to do more than what's expected, go sell everything you possess and give it to the poor."

The young ruler was very distraught because he had such great wealth. The fact is, he wasn't willing to sell all he had for the treasure.

Show Jesus that your heart's desire is to really go after God! Do more than the rules. Go after more of God. Stir up your passion to get closer to God than you've ever been in your life.

I hear people say, "Man, when I first got saved, I used to be so close to God." Have you ever said that before? "Man, we used to be so on fire when we were younger." We were? What is that telling you now?

If you really want to be like everyone else, do what they're doing. But if you want to be like Jesus, go a step further. Get the edge by doing things that no one else is doing.

For example, say the new school year has started and you're all excited to see the friends you didn't see during the summer.

As you sit down at lunch with your group of friends, you notice a new student just kind of standing around, looking for a place to sit — a place where they'll fit in. You know you should invite this new student to sit with you and your friends. Why? Because you know Jesus would. But you don't. You could have a multitude of reasons, but none of them are good reasons. If you look closely at your heart, you will probably see that the main reason is selfishness — not a characteristic of someone with the edge.

Those who have the edge examine their hearts to get rid of self so they can be full of Jesus.

If you want all of God that you can possibly have in a human body say, "God, I want it! Whatever it is, blow my mind. I want the unexpected. I want what I've never seen before. I want what I've only heard about in the Scripture!" Then get ready to see God move and operate in your life like never before!

CHECKLIST:

• • • • • • • • • • • • • •

☐ Today, read Luke 11.

☐ Is there any sin you need to repent of today?

☐ Are you grateful that God has forgiven you?

☐ Have you been talked out of any part of your Christianity?

☐ Will you give your all to Jesus today?

☐ Spend some time praising and worshipping God.

☐ Pray over your own life and your day today.

☐ Pray for your family, friends, and those in authority.

☐ Pray for the people of the world to be saved.

☐ Ask God if He wants you to go on a mission trip next summer.

☐ Do you have the edge to meet the challenges of your day?

HAVING THE EDGE

Day 3

SEEING GOD FACE-TO-FACE

So Jacob was left alone, and a man wrestled with him till daybreak.

When the man saw that he could not overpower him, he touched the socket of Jacob's hip so that his hip was wrenched as he wrestled with the man.

Then the man said, "Let me go, for it is daybreak."

But Jacob replied, "I will not let you go unless you bless me."

So Jacob called the place Peniel, saying "It is because I saw God face to face, and yet my life was spared."

Genesis 32:24-26,30

Jacob had a determination to find God and to get the blessing of God. "GOD, DON'T YOU DARE LET ME LEAVE HERE WITHOUT A BLESSING!"

Having the edge means you have regular face-to-face encounters with God and you never forget them. It's a daily encounter with Jesus Christ.

When you have the edge it gives you determination. Are you as determined as Jacob when you pray? You should go into your quiet time every day with the same kind of determination that Jacob had, declaring, "I refuse to just sit here and go through the motions! I must connect with You today, God!"

Jacob had the edge. With determination he said to the Lord, "You're not going anywhere. I want something from You!" Are you that determined? Can you imagine telling the Lord, "Do You think you're getting out of here without blessing me? You ain't going nowhere."

What is it you want from the Lord?

_____

_____

Do you have the same zeal, energy, excitement, and confidence that you had the day you were saved?

If you don't have the edge, I want you to pray this prayer with me. Choose right now to be determined like Jacob was. Break through to God this morning.

Lord Jesus, change me. I have to have the edge. I want to experience You face-to-face. I'm tired of going through the motions of a quiet time without You blessing me, filling me, and touching my life. I want Your presence and power to operate through me. I want to push past what I once thought was good and acceptable into the best You have to offer. I want to see other people's lives changed for Your glory. I want Your saving, healing, delivering power to operate in my life. Thank You for Your anointing. Thank You for using me to affect others. In Jesus' name I pray, amen.

CHECKLIST:

- [ ] Today, read Luke 12.
- [ ] Is there any sin you need to repent of today?
- [ ] Are you grateful that God has forgiven you?
- [ ] Have you been talked out of any part of your Christianity?
- [ ] Will you give your all to Jesus today?
- [ ] Spend some time praising and worshipping God.
- [ ] Pray over your own life and your day today.
- [ ] Pray for your family, friends, and those in authority.
- [ ] Pray for the people of the world to be saved.
- [ ] Ask God if He wants you to go on a mission trip next summer.
- [ ] Do you have the edge to meet the challenges of your day?

HAVING THE EDGE

Day 4

POWER TO DO WHAT IS RIGHT

Afterward Moses and Aaron went to Pharaoh and said, "This is what the Lord, the God of Israel, says: 'Let my people go.'"

Exodus 5:1

Moses had the edge. You didn't talk that boldly to Pharaoh unless you had the edge. Moses had the audacity to make such a demand, because he knew there was a God who would back him up. Moses knew he was speaking the words of the Lord.

When you have the edge, you can make a demand. The edge gives you boldness! That doesn't mean you order everyone around, but you have the confidence and the power to demand that the devil take a hike. Your prayers aren't a bunch of meaningless words timidly saying, "Now devil, you really ought to leave me alone, you know." What's up with that? Do you think that scares the devil away? When you have the edge you cry, "DEVIL, I BIND YOU IN THE NAME OF JESUS. GET OUT OF HERE!"

Shadrach, Meshach and Abednego replied to the king, "O Nebuchadnezzar, we do not need to defend ourselves before you in this matter.

"If we are thrown into the blazing furnace, the God we serve is able to save us from it, and he will rescue us from your hand, O king.

"But even if he does not, we want you to know, O king, that we will not serve your gods or worship the image of gold you have set up."

Daniel 3:16-18

Shadrach, Meshach, and Abednego had the edge. When you speak to a king like Nebuchadnezzar, you have to have the edge. No matter what decree was made, they were going to do what was right — worship their God, the only true God. Knowing full well what could possibly happen if they disobeyed the order, they didn't care. They must have experienced the power of God before this in order to tell the king that their God could deliver them from a fiery furnace. But even if they weren't delivered, they still would not worship the king's false gods.

They had the edge. It feels good when you hear it because it's so right. When you have the edge you can stake your life on it, because you have the Giver of life living inside of you. When you have the edge you know it's God — you know it's the truth. It's the cutting edge of reality. The edge gives you courage!

Put yourself in a similar situation these four men were in. You may not have to go before Pharaohs and kings, but you may have to take a stand for God before other people in your life, such as your friends, teachers, or coaches.

Are you like Moses, Shadrach, Meshach, and Abednego?

Are you willing to put your life on the line to do what is right in the sight of God?

Have your friends ever asked you to do something with them that you knew wasn't right? If so, what did you do?

_____

_____

Has a teacher ever given you an assignment that contradicts the Christian faith? If so, what did you do?

_____

CHECKLIST:
• • • • • • • • • • • • •

☐ Today, read Luke 13.

☐ Is there any sin you need to repent of today?

☐ Are you grateful that God has forgiven you?

☐ Have you been talked out of any part of your Christianity?

☐ Will you give your all to Jesus today?

☐ Spend some time praising and worshipping God.

☐ Pray over your own life and your day today.

☐ Pray for your family, friends, and those in authority.

☐ Pray for the people of the world to be saved.

☐ Ask God if He wants you to go on a mission trip next summer.

☐ Do you have the edge to meet the challenges of your day?

_____

_____

Has a coach pressured you into playing "dirty ball"? If so, what did you do?

_____

_____

_____

_____

_____

If you have the edge, you have the power to stand up and say, "I will do what is right — no matter what anyone thinks and no matter what it costs me."

Remember: The Spirit of God lives IN YOU! You have the power to do what is right!

HAVING THE EDGE

Day 5

HAVING THE FIRE

But if I say, "I will not mention him or speak any more in his name," his word is in my heart like a fire, a fire shut up in my bones. I am weary of holding it in; indeed, I cannot.

Jeremiah 20:9

Jeremiah had the edge. The Word of God was like fire in his bones. He couldn't keep his mouth shut. He just had to tell people about God!

When you have the edge you have *fire*. You have a word that's burning in your heart and you say, "I can't keep this to myself. It's like a fire raging inside of me."

Yet when I preach the gospel, I cannot boast, for I am compelled to preach. Woe to me if I do not preach the gospel.

1 Corinthians 9:16

Paul's attitude was, *I've got to preach this thing! If I don't, I won't be able to live with myself. It's real! It's alive! The gospel message is so real that if I don't preach it, I'll be miserable!* Paul had a fire that burned in his bones. It was a deep, overwhelming conviction. To not minister the Gospel was agony to Paul. When you have the edge you have a tremendous conviction in your heart and your mind that you must do all you can do to see people saved.

A lot of people have good teaching but no real fire — and that disturbs me. One of the worst insults is when someone comes up to me after a service and says, "That was a real neat sermon." I don't want anyone telling me I had a *neat* sermon. I want my sermons to be full of fire. I want to see people's lives transformed by the power of Almighty God. I want them so stunned that they forgot they were on earth. I want them so transported to where they're not even able to speak, because they just had an encounter with God. If they're coherent enough to know that it was a neat teaching, then I must not have had the edge.

Do you have that kind of conviction every time you can share the Gospel?

Does a fire burn in your bones to share Jesus with your friends?

If you can't say that, my challenge to you is to purpose in your heart to have this kind of conviction. "IF I DON'T SPEAK THIS, I'LL DIE! I'VE GOT TO. IT'S SO REAL. IT'S SO RIGHT! Woe to me, if I don't."

If you don't have this kind of conviction this morning, cry out to God. Go after the edge! Approach your day with the same zeal Paul had every day: "If I don't stand up for Jesus today, if I don't live what I believe, it will eat me alive on the inside! I have got to share the truth!"

CHECKLIST:
• • • • • • • • • • • • • • • •

- [ ] Today, read Luke 14.
- [ ] Is there any sin you need to repent of today?
- [ ] Are you grateful that God has forgiven you?
- [ ] Have you been talked out of any part of your Christianity?
- [ ] Will you give your all to Jesus today?
- [ ] Spend some time praising and worshipping God.
- [ ] Pray over your own life and your day today.
- [ ] Pray for your family, friends, and those in authority.
- [ ] Pray for the people of the world to be saved.
- [ ] Ask God if He wants you to go on a mission trip next summer.
- [ ] Do you have the edge to meet the challenges of your day?

HAVING THE EDGE

Day 6

CONFIDENCE TO SPEAK THE TRUTH

Then Elijah said to them, "I am the only one of the Lord's prophets left, but Baal has four hundred and fifty prophets.

"Get two bulls for us. Let them choose one for themselves, and let them cut it into pieces and put it on the wood but not set fire to it. I will prepare the other bull and put it on the wood but not set fire to it.

"Then you call on the name of your god, and I will call on the name of the Lord. The god who answers by fire — he is God."

1 Kings 18:22-24

It was Elijah and God against Baal and his 450 prophets. Elijah and God were the majority and Elijah knew it. He didn't back down. He didn't succumb to peer pressure. Elijah had the edge. Not only did God answer by fire, but the fire of God was in Elijah. When you have the edge, you have the confidence of Elijah.

John the Baptist had the edge.

But when he saw many of the Pharisees and Sadducees coming to where he was baptizing, he said to them: "You brood of vipers! Who warned you to flee from the coming wrath?

"Produce fruit in keeping with repentance.

"And do not think you can say to yourselves, 'We have Abraham as our father.' I tell you that out of these stones God can raise up children for Abraham.

"The ax is already at the root of the trees, and every tree that does not produce good fruit will be cut down and thrown into the fire.

"I baptize you with water for repentance. But after me will come one who is more powerful than I, whose sandals I am not fit to carry. He will baptize you with the Holy Spirit and with fire.

"His winnowing fork is in his hand, and he will clear his threshing floor, gathering the wheat into the barn and burning up the chaff with unquenchable fire."

Matthew 3:7-12

John the Baptist looked at the rulers — the religious people of that day — and said, "You're just a bunch of snakes! I warned you to get your life right. Change your life and show some fruit of repentance!" When you have the edge, you have confidence to proclaim what's right. You speak the Word of God and it thunders.

We've been told since our early Sunday school days about David slaying Goliath with just a few smooth rocks and a sling-shot. But David had the edge.

David said to the Philistine, "You come against me with sword and spear and javelin, but I come against you in the name of the Lord Almighty, the God of the armies of Israel, whom you have defied.

"This day the Lord will hand you over to me, and I'll strike you down and cut off your head. Today I will give the carcasses of the Philistine army to the birds of the air and the beasts of the earth, and the whole world will know that there is a God in Israel.

"All those gathered here will know that it is not by sword or spear that the Lord saves; for the battle is the Lord's, and he will give all of you into our hands."

1 Samuel 17:45-47

Can you image the confidence David had to speak to Goliath that way? You don't tell a giant that you're going to cut off his head and feed his dead body to the birds without having the edge.

Elijah, John the Baptist, and David saw God come on the scene in powerful ways. But these were not one-time events. Study different men and women of the Old Testament, like Queen Esther, Hosea, and Jonah, and see how they had the edge. See how God strengthened them for the task at hand. Their confidence was in the Lord God Almighty and nothing was going to weaken them.

Are you in a situation that you're needing the confidence of the Lord?

Ask the Lord for a supernatural bold-ness to proclaim truth and do what is right. Then write down what happened.

_____

_____

_____

_____

_____

_____

CHECKLIST:

• • • • • • • • • • • •

- [ ] Today, read Luke 15 and 16.
- [ ] Is there any sin you need to repent of today?
- [ ] Are you grateful that God has forgiven you?
- [ ] Have you been talked out of any part of your Christianity?
- [ ] Will you give your all to Jesus today?
- [ ] Spend some time praising and worship-ping God.
- [ ] Pray over your own life and your day today.
- [ ] Pray for your family, friends, and those in authority.
- [ ] Pray for the people of the world to be saved.
- [ ] Ask God if He wants you to go on a mission trip next summer.
- [ ] Do you have the edge to meet the challenges of your day?

137
• • • •

HAVING THE EDGE

Day 7

HOW DO YOU KNOW YOU HAVE THE EDGE?

"Therefore let all Israel be assured of this: God has made this Jesus, whom you crucified, both Lord and Christ."
When the people heard this, they were cut to the heart and said to Peter and the other apostles, "Brothers, what shall we do?"

Acts 2:36,37

Peter had the edge. This was a crowd of 3000 people who were cut to the heart by his sermon. They desperately wanted to know how to be saved. They wanted to know Jesus in a real way.

When you have the edge, people's hearts get pierced by your words and by your life. They're not the same. Your witness grips their life. They have to respond. You know you have the edge when your witness cuts the hearts of people.

Think about the concept of being "on the edge." If you have a crowd of people and you're not on the edge, you're in the middle. When you're in the middle, no one notices you because you're not much different than anyone else. But when you get to the edge, it separates you from the masses.

That is what having the edge is all about.

What is the edge? You know you have the edge when you know God. I mean, God is all over your words and all over your life. He's all over you. You know you have the edge when you have the right word at the right time, and you think, "Mmm, that felt so good preaching that! They got it!" You saw how they responded.

To be a leader in your generation, you've got to have something stirring inside you that is so powerful you cannot keep your mouth shut. There are lots of people who have a position, but they have nothing stirring inside them. They got into that position because they wanted recognition, but they've got nothing of God burning inside them to give to others. There's no fresh manna.

Are you in a position of leadership?

Even if you aren't in an official leadership position, God wants you to lead your generation.

You lead when you influence others. Make a list of some people you might influence today and how the edge will help you.

_____

_____

_____

How can you keep the edge?

_____

_____

CHECKLIST:
• • • • • • • • • • • •

☐ Today, read Luke 17 and 18.

☐ Is there any sin you need to repent of today?

☐ Are you grateful that God has forgiven you?

☐ Have you been talked out of any part of your Christianity?

☐ Will you give your all to Jesus today?

☐ Spend some time praising and worshipping God.

☐ Pray over your own life and your day today.

☐ Pray for your family, friends, and those in authority.

☐ Pray for the people of the world to be saved.

☐ Ask God if He wants you to go on a mission trip next summer.

☐ Do you have the edge to meet the challenges of your day?

chapter 8

HAVE YOU LOST THE EDGE?

For Demas has forsaken me,
having loved this present world.

2 Timothy 4:10 KJV

Day 1

DOES THE TERM "RADICAL" DESCRIBE YOU?

Obviously we all have different personalities. But when you are passionate about something — you get radical. You go to the extreme.

What do you get radical about? Are you radical about your football or basketball team at school? I've gone to high school games and have watched even the shyest people stand up, yell, shout, scream, and practically make fools of themselves — all in the spirit of a ball game.

But those same "outgoing" football fanatics look like they're attending a funeral when they're at church. They sit in their pew with a long, if not bored, face and they just sort of mumble the words during the praise and worship time. I want to walk up to them, shake them, and say, "Where's the passion and fervor I saw in you at the ball game Friday night?"

Many people raised in church have been conditioned to be

very sober, solemn, and quiet in church. Why? Are we afraid we'll wake God up? Maybe some noise in those churches just might scare the devil away! We are going to be rejoicing, singing, and dancing around the throne room of God throughout all of eternity. There is no timidity in heaven. We might as well start preparing ourselves right now.

Hopefully, we've all been in church services where people are shouting "Amen," the preacher is on fire, the choir is dancing, and everyone around is excited. You think, *Man, if this is what heaven is like, this is gonna be fun!"*

Now obviously, there are some sermons that aren't shouting sermons — they may be convicting sermons. But even when it's convicting, there's still something you know is right. When those words cut to the depths of your heart you still think, *I wish more people preached like this.* Then you've been in services before that were nice, but it was just another sermon. It was good teaching, but it was missing the fire. There was no thunder to it.

Do you consider yourself to be a radical Christian? If you're not radical for Jesus, what is there that's worth being radical about?

_____

When your name comes up in conversation, what is said about you?

_____

Do you tell others about Jesus every chance you get?

List some ways you can become more radical for Jesus.

_____

_____

CHECKLIST:

- [ ] Today, read Luke 19.
- [ ] Is there any sin you need to repent of today?
- [ ] Are you grateful that God has forgiven you?
- [ ] Have you been talked out of any part of your Christianity?
- [ ] Will you give your all to Jesus today?
- [ ] Spend some time praising and worshipping God.
- [ ] Pray over your own life and your day today.
- [ ] Pray for your family, friends, and those in authority.
- [ ] Pray for the people of the world to be saved.
- [ ] Ask God if He wants you to go on a mission trip next summer.
- [ ] Do you have the edge to meet the challenges of your day?

HAVE YOU LOST THE EDGE?

Day 2

YOU KNOW YOU'VE LOST THE EDGE WHEN...

…you don't tell your unsaved friends about Jesus for fear of being uncool.

…you think you can go through your day without a time alone with God.

…you say you love Jesus, but you have no passion to serve Him.

…you want to minister, but you won't press deeper into the things of God.

…you issue a challenge, but have no conviction, so you never follow through.

…you live by your emotions and thinking instead of God's Word.

…your emotions are ruled by circumstances rather than by the promises of God.

...you are not continually aware of the leading and voice of the Holy Spirit.

...you go to church, but the Holy Spirit never touches and changes you.

...you look good on the outside, but your heart is far from God.

You may say a little prayer, "Oh God, please bless my day and help me on my algebra test," — as you are walking into math class. But you don't have a special time to spend in prayer, just pressing into God and listening to Him, getting the answers and direction you need for the day.

If you don't sense God's presence every second of the day, it's no big deal anymore. You're doing okay on your own. Then, if God does show up, you are surprised. You nod a thanks to Him and you are on your way again — your own way, not His way. But actually, by this time you don't even know that it's your way and not His way. By this time you have bought the lie that you're okay living the way you are living.

Then one day after school, you see a girl alone at her locker, crying. You ask her what's the matter and she tells you she's pregnant and doesn't know what to do. She figures she'll just get an abortion like everyone else, says it's no big deal, it's happened to so many, and she feels stupid she's so upset.

Instead of telling her about Jesus, His forgiveness and His life-changing power, and how He loves her and already loves the baby she's carrying, you mumble something like, "Gee, that's really awful, uh, well, I'll uh, pray for you. Good luck!" Then you run out the door and can't wait to call your best friend with the gossip — unless the friend is a Christian, in which case you tell them they need to pray for her because....

These are not the only ways to know you have lost your edge. You may be able to come up with a few more of your own. Can you list them?

---

have you lost the edge?

••••••••••••••••••••••••••••••

you know you've lost the edge when...

_____

_____

_____

_____

CHECKLIST:

•••••••••••••••••

☐ Today, read Luke 20.

☐ Is there any sin you need to repent of today?

☐ Are you grateful that God has forgiven you?

☐ Have you been talked out of any part of your Christianity?

☐ Will you give your all to Jesus today?

☐ Spend some time praising and worshipping God.

☐ Pray over your own life and your day today.

☐ Pray for your family, friends, and those in authority.

☐ Pray for the people of the world to be saved.

☐ Ask God if He wants you to go on a mission trip next summer.

☐ Do you have the edge to meet the challenges of your day?

Would you have to say that any of these things describe you? If so, what steps do you need to take to get the edge back in your life?

_____

_____

_____

_____

_____

_____

_____

_____

HAVE YOU LOST THE EDGE?

Day 3
. . . .

RESULTS OF LOSING THE EDGE

There's a certain limit to which you cannot sin against God, ask forgiveness, and everything's okay again. Yes, He'll forgive you. But there comes a time that we cheat ourselves out of what God truly has for us.

Take another look at Moses. This guy met with God on the mountain. He had a direct, personal conversation with Almighty God. But one day Moses got hacked off at the people for their rebellion and struck a rock. (See Numbers 20:1-13.) We think, *Why was that so horrible? All he did was get mad and hit a rock.* But because Moses did not trust and honor God as holy in front of the people, he didn't get to experience all that God had originally planned for him. He missed the promised land.

The people he was leading didn't do so well either. God delivered them from slavery in Egypt, saved them from Pharaoh's army by parting the Red Sea, gave them food and water in the wilderness, and saw that they always were warm at night and had shelter from the sun during the day. Yet, when they came to the promised land they had no faith in Him to give them victory over their enemies in order to take it. The Bible uses them as an example for us NOT to follow:

Therefore, since the promise of entering his rest still stands, let us be careful that none of you be found to have fallen short of it.

For we also have had the gospel preached to us, just as they did; but the message they heard was of no value to them, because those who heard did not combine it with faith.

Now we who have believed enter that rest, just as God has said, "So I declared on oath in my anger, 'They shall never enter my rest.'"

Hebrews 4:1-3

That entire generation was kept from entering the land promised to them because they did not believe God's Word. The truth is, they were afraid. So Moses lost his temper and the children of Israel got scared, but God forgave them and still loved them. Nevertheless, only two of them got the special blessing of entering the promised land — Joshua and Caleb. Joshua and Caleb were the only two who believed and honored God.

God expected more out of Moses and the children of Israel because they had a special relationship. In Moses' case, they had a very personal relationship. When you have the edge, and you can only have the edge when you have a very intimate relationship with God, you can't get away with things that the average Joe Christian gets away with!

That's one reason why I will always be faithful to my wife and stay honest in my ministry. I love having a great family life, and I love having the opportunity to really affect a life by the Spirit of God, and I don't want to risk losing all that God has for me by continuing to sin. It's not that God wouldn't forgive, because He forgives all the time. But something happens when you're close to God and you make that decision to step into sin — when you don't trust God completely and you don't honor

Him as holy. You lose something as a consequence, and it is very difficult and sometimes impossible to get the edge back.

"You are the salt of the earth. But if the salt loses its saltiness, how can it be made salty again? It is no longer good for anything, except to be thrown out and trampled by men."

Matthew 5:13

What is salt good for if it isn't salty? It's useless and we throw it away. The interesting thing about losing the edge is that we think no one notices, but everyone notices. If we lose the edge, we are no longer the salt of the earth. We can no longer affect people's lives.

Don't lose the edge! List three ways you can be the salt of the earth.

1. _____

_____

2. _____

_____

3. _____

_____

Now do your checklist to stay salty!

CHECKLIST:

☐ Today, read Luke 21.

☐ Is there any sin you need to repent of today?

☐ Are you grateful that God has forgiven you?

☐ Have you been talked out of any part of your Christianity?

☐ Will you give your all to Jesus today?

☐ Spend some time praising and worshipping God.

☐ Pray over your own life and your day today.

☐ Pray for your family, friends, and those in authority.

☐ Pray for the people of the world to be saved.

☐ Ask God if He wants you to go on a mission trip next summer.

☐ Do you have the edge to meet the challenges of your day?

Have You Lost the Edge?

Day 4
• •

CAN YOU LOSE THE EDGE
AND KEEP THE ANOINTING?

A certain man of Zorah, named Manoah, from the clan of the Danites, had a wife who was sterile and remained childless.

The angel of the Lord appeared to her and said, "You are sterile and childless, but you are going to conceive and have a son.

"Now see to it that you drink no wine or other fermented drink and that you do not eat anything unclean,

"Because you will conceive and give birth to a son. No razor may be used on his head, because the boy is to be a Nazarite, set apart to God from birth, and he will begin the deliverance of Israel from the hands of the Philistines."

Judges 13:2-5

Samson was destined to be very special and used by God in a very mighty way. Can you imagine an angel telling your mother that you were going to be born so you could deliver an entire nation from the enemy? Samson had the edge before he was even born!

Samson had quite a life. He married a Philistine woman who betrayed him. When she was given to Samson's friend to be his wife, Samson killed the Philistines for revenge, and the Philistines in turn burned his wife and her father. (See Judges 13-15.) The Philistines hated Samson with a passion.

Judges 16:1 tells us that he began seeing a prostitute named Delilah in Gaza. By this time he was a leader in Israel. So here's Samson, who was committed to the Lord his whole life and is a leader in Israel, sleeping with a prostitute!

The people of Gaza told the Philistines Samson was visiting Delilah, but he escaped by getting up in the middle of the night, grabbing the doors at the city gate which weighed a ton, tearing them loose, and carrying them to the top of a hill. That can't be done with average human strength. It had to be a supernatural, God-given strength.

How could God allow this? This guy's acting like a total heathen. He's a backslider who's in extreme sin!

For the gifts and calling of God are without repentance.

Romans 11:29 KJV

This verse is one of the most important to understand to keep the edge. God is warning us, "Look, I gave you talents, abilities, and a mission on this earth. You will always have these, whether you're a believer or not, whether your heart is right with Me or not. So don't be fooled when you sin and the gifts are still there and the doors to do what I called you to do still open. The wages of sin is ultimately still death!" (See Romans 3:23.)

You can walk through the doors and use your talents and gifts while you're sinning in some area of your life, but if you do not allow the Spirit and the Word of God to deal with that sin and you don't get the help you need to get rid of it, it will eventually

have you lost the edge?
● ●
can you lose the edge and keep the anointing?

destroy your life. And the first thing that happens when you start on this path of destruction is that you lose the edge.

You only have the edge when your heart, soul, mind, and strength totally belong to God.

If you lose the edge, you will eventually lose the anointing. When you lose the anointing, you end up doing everything by your own ability — you have no power. Don't play with sin thinking, *God forgives me. Hey, it's okay.* It's not okay and it's not worth losing the edge!

Are you involved in sinful activity that could cause you to lose the edge?

What are some areas you need to commit to the Lord so He can strengthen you?

_____

_____

_____

_____

_____

_____

CHECKLIST:
● ● ● ● ● ● ● ● ● ● ● ●

☐ Today, read Luke 22.

☐ Is there any sin you need to repent of today?

☐ Are you grateful that God has forgiven you?

☐ Have you been talked out of any part of your Christianity?

☐ Will you give your all to Jesus today?

☐ Spend some time praising and worshipping God.

☐ Pray over your own life and your day today.

☐ Pray for your family, friends, and those in authority.

☐ Pray for the people of the world to be saved.

☐ Ask God if He wants you to go on a mission trip next summer.

☐ Do you have the edge to meet the challenges of your day?

Day 5

THE DESTRUCTION OF SAMSON

The Philistines knew Samson had a thing for Delilah, so they offered her money if she could find out the secret to his power.

So Delilah said to Samson, "Tell me the secret of your great strength and how you can be tied up and subdued."

Samson answered her, "If anyone ties me with seven fresh thongs that have not been dried, I'll become as weak as any other man."

Judges 16:6,7

Samson was toying with Delilah, but Delilah did not take this as a joke. After he went to sleep, she tied him with seven fresh thongs, then woke him up and said, "Samson, the Philistines are here! Wake up!" Boom! He busted the thongs off.

Now I don't know about you, but if I was Samson, I would be thinking, *Hey, maybe I need to check to see if she's really sincere. I don't know if she loves me for who I am.* But Delilah headed him off at the pass by accusing him of not really loving her.

The next night she asked him again what the source of his strength was, and this time he told her that if he was tied up with seven fresh ropes he would be as weak as any other man. So of course, she did that and then yelled, "Samson, wake up! The Philistines are here!" Boom! He breaks loose again. She gets mad and accuses him of not loving her.

Now I'm thinking, *Samson, what do you have in your head? How could you be so stupid?* That was the second time she betrayed him and the second time she made him feel guilty about it. Talk about losing the edge! When you lose the edge you do some incredibly stupid things and don't even realize it.

The third time around, Samson told her that if she would weave the seven braids of his hair into a fabric in the loom and tighten it with a pin, he would become as weak as any other man. So while he was sleeping, Delilah did just that. (Personally, I don't know how Samson slept through it!) Then again she cried out, "Wake up, Samson!"

Samson threw the loom all over the room and she said, "Oh great, you lied to me again!" Now I'm thinking, *Three times Samson! What's up, man?* Talk about being dense! Talk about losing the edge! Samson was supposed to be this anointed man of Israel and he couldn't see what was happening right in front of his face. This is what happens when you lose the edge.

Finally he told her the true secret to his power — never cutting his hair. So what did Delilah do? She cut his hair and he lost the edge. The Philistines gouged out his eyes, chained him, and used him to grind grain. (See Judges 16.) Samson is a portrait of someone who lost the edge and didn't even realize it.

You go through your little Christian activities and everything looks good, but bit by bit you begin to lose the edge. You begin to lose the fervency you once had for the Lord. You begin to lose the passion to see people saved and hearts and lives changed. Sadly, it can happen so gradually that you don't even realize the edge is diminishing until it's gone.

have you lost the edge?
● ●
the destruction of Samson

Are there any sins you are justifying or making excuses for?

Are there any areas in your life where you are compromising?

If you said yes to either of these questions, get on your face right now and submit yourself to God. Tell Him everything, get forgiven and cleansed, and then ask Him for the strength and wisdom to keep from falling for the same thing again. Don't be stupid like Samson! Keep the edge!

Today, set your heart to get these issues straight with God:

_____

_____

_____

_____

_____

_____

_____

_____

CHECKLIST:
● ● ● ● ● ● ● ● ● ● ● ●

☐ Today, read Luke 23.

☐ Is there any sin you need to repent of today?

☐ Are you grateful that God has forgiven you?

☐ Have you been talked out of any part of your Christianity?

☐ Will you give your all to Jesus today?

☐ Spend some time praising and worshipping God.

☐ Pray over your own life and your day today.

☐ Pray for your family, friends, and those in authority.

☐ Pray for the people of the world to be saved.

☐ Ask God if He wants you to go on a mission trip next summer.

☐ Do you have the edge to meet the challenges of your day?

Have You Lost the Edge?

Day 6

MATURITY IS THE EDGE

What ideas pop in your head when you think of a mature Christian? Do you think of the little old lady down the street who never goes anywhere except to church? Do you think of someone who has a list of rules in their pocket, ready at a moment's notice to pull them out and recite them?

A mature Christian is one who hears and obeys the Word of God, seeks after Him in all their ways, and commits every part of their life to Him. I didn't say they were perfect, I said they were mature. They have the edge because they are always growing in their relationship with God. They know it is a process.

Like newborn babies, crave pure spiritual milk, so that by it you may grow up in your salvation.

1 Peter 2:2

A newborn baby has no teeth, so all they can have is milk. They rely solely on their mother because they can't feed themselves. Spiritually, a newborn Christian is the same way. They sit in church and take the milk from the pastor, because they can't feed themselves. They are learning the basics of the Christian faith. What's good about this level is that they *crave* the milk. Newborns cry when they are hungry. Are you that hungry for God? Do you cry, "Oh God, feed me! I want more of You!"

But solid food is for the mature, who by constant use have trained themselves to distinguish good from evil.

Hebrews 5:14

One of the signs of maturity in the Lord is your response to the meat. When you hear a sermon that convicts your heart, or if someone confronts you about something in your life, what do you do? A mature Christian will deal with any area of sin in their life to keep the edge. In most cases they don't even need a special message from God, because during their time of prayer and Bible study, they let the Holy Spirit do His work in them.

When you have the edge, you don't sit in church with the attitude of, *Feed me, pray for me, take care of me.* Your attitude has become, *Father, give me everything I need and change anything that needs to be changed so that I can minister to others.*

Unfortunately, there are many Christians who've had the spiritual milk and maybe just a taste of the meat, so now they think they know what it's all about. This is *spiritual arrogance.* They're so caught up with their own level of *knowledge,* they forget Christianity is about *people.* Jesus died for people.

You have the edge when you have an attitude of love, not self-centeredness.

So how do you get from the milk level to the solid food level and avoid spiritual arrogance?

For this very reason, make every effort to add to your faith goodness; and to goodness, knowledge;

And to knowledge, self-control; and to self-control, perseverance; and to perseverance, godliness;

And to godliness, brotherly kindness; and to brotherly kindness, love.

For if you possess these qualities in increasing measure, they will keep you from being ineffective and unproductive in your knowledge of our Lord Jesus Christ.

But if anyone does not have them, he is nearsighted and blind, and has forgotten that he has been cleansed from his past sins.

2 Peter 1:5-9

CHECKLIST:

- ☐ Today, read Luke 24 and John 1.
- ☐ Is there any sin you need to repent of today?
- ☐ Are you grateful that God has forgiven you?
- ☐ Have you been talked out of any part of your Christianity?
- ☐ Will you give your all to Jesus today?
- ☐ Spend some time praising and worshipping God.
- ☐ Pray over your own life and your day today.
- ☐ Pray for your family, friends, and those in authority.
- ☐ Pray for the people of the world to be saved.
- ☐ Ask God if He wants you to go on a mission trip next summer.
- ☐ Do you have the edge to meet the challenges of your day?

Have you forgotten you were cleansed from your sins? Have you forgotten you're saved, you're a child of God? Do you really hunger and thirst after Him enough to let the Holy Spirit develop all these great qualities in your life? God wants to show you in His Word how to live, grow, prosper, and change the world. Then you won't just make a little dent in your school; you'll start a revolution! When you have the edge, you do what God's Word and His Spirit tell you.

Read the list of qualities in 2 Peter 1:5-7 again. Which ones are your strengths?

_____

_____

_____

Which ones are your weaknesses, and what do you need to do about them?

_____

_____

_____

HAVE YOU LOST THE EDGE?

Day 7

FROM GLORY TO GLORY

But we all, with open face beholding as in a glass the glory of the Lord, are changed into the same image from glory to glory, even as by the Spirit of the Lord.

2 Corinthians 3:18 KJV

Every experience with God is terrific and life-changing, but we cannot live from one experience to the next. To keep the edge we must go from glory to glory, and that means every day we are spending time with God and letting Him change us and direct us. If we have a profound, life-changing experience, that's great! But what we live for is simply living in the presence of God and following after Jesus.

If you live for experiences, things can get really out of focus and you can even stop growing. Whole denominations have been built on *one* experience. God showed up on the scene, He blew people's minds, and for the next ten years they preached about it and sang about it. "Oh, wasn't that exciting? Remember that day?" And no one grows beyond that one experience.

But what about us today? Don't we do the same thing? We want to be in *the happening* youth group. There's nothing wrong with being in a great youth group — I want you to be as involved in it as you can be — but when we get the least bit bored with what's happening, we're off and running to find another youth group with more zing, more excitement, and more fun.

Or we have a supernatural spiritual experience with God at camp and we build our Christian life around that one experience. We think that if we don't have a similar experience every week in youth group, we're not experiencing God. So we pray, "Oh God, I want that same fire, Lord. Rain it down again, just like at camp!" When a little bit of fire comes from heaven — *whoosh!* "Oh, I'm so blessed. Ahh." Then we're back at it again, "God, give me a little fire like before, please!"

So we experience a little bit of revival. It's precious. It's awesome. It's the best. It's like nothing ever before. And then it passes. So we start asking for something like it again and hope the next meeting, or the next camp, or the next concert, or the next convention, is going to be what brings a little more fire.

We go from experience to experience — from jolt to jolt — and become experience-oriented, rather than cultivating and kindling a fire that really stays burning. We keep that fire burning through a personal relationship with Jesus Christ, and that relationship is based on the Word of God and prayer.

Getting the edge and keeping it means that you can't just go through the motions reading your Bible and praying. You have to really see God with all your heart as you read. This will make you mature in the Lord — not just going from one experience to another.

God is not there to give us one experience after another so we can keep our edge. He's there to live our lives with us! He wants to love us, bless us, instruct us, teach us, warn us of danger, tell us how to defeat our enemies, give us wisdom to do everything He's called us to do and be the person He created us to be.

A daily intimate relationship with the Father is the greatest experience!

When we rely on experiences, it's easy to get bland and begin to go through the motions. It's easy to get stale in our relationship with God. For example, say you had a mega-revival in your life. I mean, the fire fell! It was incredible! It was awesome! And in the middle of it, you're thinking, *God, You're just so great!*

I'll never be the same. I'm free of all these bad habits. I'll never think a bad thought the rest of my life. I'm practically raptured right now!

The next morning you wake up and think, *Where did God go? How come I'm having a bad thought? Oh man, was it real? Maybe it wasn't real after all.* That's because you're relying on an experience instead of God — and the experience is gone. The thing you have to remember is that GOD ISN'T GONE!

God is the One Who brings the fire, so just walk with Him.

We should be saying, "God, I want to go from glory to glory. I want Your fire to burn in me day and night. I don't want a little flash. I want the real thing. Don't just give me an experience, give me a *lifestyle.*"

Now don't misunderstand me — when you first meet Jesus and He is real to you, that is an experience you should remember every day of your life. That's when Jesus became real to you and from that moment on no one could talk you out of it. But as you grow more mature in the Lord, you keep the edge by experiencing God every moment of every day in relationship.

Have you been going from experience to experience?

Stop now and decide to get the edge back by going from glory to glory. Get involved in your local church. Get involved in your youth group. There may only be five kids there, but if those five are on fire for God, you can change your community and your school. It's okay to visit other youth groups every once in a while, but your youth pastor needs to know you are *committed* to your youth group.

List four ways you can show your commitment to your youth group.

_____

_____

_____

CHECKLIST:
· · · · · · · · · · · · · · ·

☐ Today, read John 2 and 3.

☐ Is there any sin you need to repent of today?

☐ Are you grateful that God has forgiven you?

☐ Have you been talked out of any part of your Christianity?

☐ Will you give your all to Jesus today?

☐ Spend some time praising and worshipping God.

☐ Pray over your own life and your day today.

☐ Pray for your family, friends, and those in authority.

☐ Pray for the people of the world to be saved.

☐ Ask God if He wants you to go on a mission trip next summer.

☐ Do you have the edge to meet the challenges of your day?

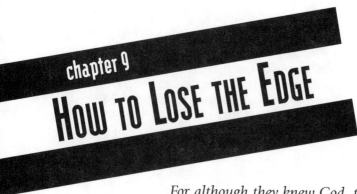

chapter 9

How to Lose the Edge

*For although they knew God, they neither
glorified him as God nor gave thanks to him,
but their thinking became futile and their
foolish hearts were darkened. Although they
claimed to be wise, they became fools.*

Romans 1:21,22

Day 1

SIN

Put to death, therefore, whatever belongs to your earthly nature: sexual immorality, impurity, lust, evil desires and greed, which is idolatry.

Because of these, the wrath of God is coming.

You used to walk in these ways, in the life you once lived.

But now you must rid yourselves of all such things as these: anger, rage, malice, slander, and filthy language from your lips.

Colossians 3:5-8

God wants us to deal with sin the moment it shows its ugly face. If we justify our sinful behavior or compromise our beliefs, we will lose the edge. It doesn't even take a big sin. If we are walking in sin of any kind, we will lose the edge.

We can be deceived like Samson. He didn't lose the edge the first or even the second time he sinned. Look at all the things he got away with before he died. But at what price? To confide in someone who didn't love him — was that the best God had for his life? We think, *It's okay to fool around, or not to have quiet time, or to watch too much TV, or to see the dirty movie. I mean, I've been doing that for weeks now and God's still answering my prayers when I pray for people.* You are deceiving yourself!

When you walk in sin, complacency sets in. You have an *I don't care* attitude about everything — a total lack of concern. If you have the edge, you are on fire for God and you are awesomely zealous for the things of God. There is not a complacent bone in your body! You want to win people's hearts to the Lord! You want to see lives changed! You want to see bad situations turned around! Now how can you desire to see all that if you don't care about anything but watching TV and going out with your boyfriend or girlfriend?

Sin produces a hard heart. (Read Romans, chapter 1.) This goes beyond not caring. A hard heart is in outright rebellion toward God. A person with a hardened heart totally disregards what the Bible says about anything. They even think biblical views on morality are pretty absurd.

When you get a hard heart, you have totally lost the edge — and you probably don't even know it.

What is the condition of your heart today? Use your checklist to answer.

_____

_____

_____

CHECKLIST:
• • • • • • • • • • • • • • • •

☐ Today, read John 4.

☐ Is there any sin you need to repent of today?

☐ Are you grateful that God has forgiven you?

☐ Have you been talked out of any part of your Christianity?

☐ Will you give your all to Jesus today?

☐ Spend some time praising and worshipping God.

☐ Pray over your own life and your day today.

☐ Pray for your family, friends, and those in authority.

☐ Pray for the people of the world to be saved.

☐ Ask God if He wants you to go on a mission trip next summer.

☐ Do you have the edge to meet the challenges of your day?

How to Lose the Edge

DISOBEYING THE HOLY SPIRIT

"If you love me, you will obey what I command.

"And I will ask the Father, and he will give you another Counselor to be with you forever —

"The Spirit of truth. The world cannot accept him, because it neither sees him nor knows him. But you know him, for he lives with you and will be in you.

"But the Counselor, the Holy Spirit, whom the Father will send in my name, will teach you all things and will remind you of everything I have said to you."

John 14:15-17,26

Not heeding what the Holy Spirit tells you about certain things is another way to lose the edge. When the Holy Spirit convicts you about some area in your life, you need to take care of it right away. If it is sin, repent, get rid of it, and accept God's forgiveness. If you are to do something for God, go do it. The good thing is that God will give you the strength to do whatever it is. Ignoring the Holy Spirit — or not asking for His help — is the fast road to losing the edge.

Being involved in ministry, I have come across ministers who have ignored the convictions of the Holy Spirit and fallen into sin or gone the wrong direction. You may not be able to tell at first, because they are still preaching powerful sermons or singing anointed songs. But eventually their disobedience catches up with them and they lose the edge.

Some are still in the ministry today and they have nice messages, but it's not the same as it was before they disobeyed. I don't sense the *fire*. Their words seem hollow. And I think, *Just how much more powerful would these people be if they hadn't fallen into sin? How many more lives would they be affecting if they had listened to and obeyed the conviction of the Holy Spirit?*

I want to be used in the greatest way I possibly can for the kingdom of God. I want God to look at me and say, "My good and faithful servant in whom I am well pleased." I don't want to do *anything* to risk losing that. Do you?

It's not just pastors or ministers in the limelight who need to be careful. *You* need to make sure you always listen to the convictions and promptings of the Holy Spirit. If you are convicted about seeing certain types of movies, you need to heed that conviction.

Don't preach your personal conviction and don't condemn others if they don't have the same convictions, but if your friends pressure you to go along with them, don't give in. Abide by your convictions. It may be difficult at first, but the more you obey the Holy Spirit, the easier it gets.

When we disobey the Holy Spirit, it's more difficult to hear His voice the next time. Then time after time of disobedience leads to total deception. We have lost the edge and don't even know it. So listen to the Holy Spirit!

Make a list of five things the Holy Spirit has convicted you about.

1. _____

   _____

2. _____

   _____

3. _____

CHECKLIST:

- ☐ Today, read John 5.
- ☐ Is there any sin you need to repent of today?
- ☐ Are you grateful that God has forgiven you?
- ☐ Have you been talked out of any part of your Christianity?
- ☐ Will you give your all to Jesus today?
- ☐ Spend some time praising and worshipping God.
- ☐ Pray over your own life and your day today.
- ☐ Pray for your family, friends, and those in authority.
- ☐ Pray for the people of the world to be saved.
- ☐ Ask God if He wants you to go on a mission trip next summer.
- ☐ Do you have the edge to meet the challenges of your day?

4. _____

   _____

   _____

   _____

5. _____

   _____

   _____

How to Lose the Edge

Day 3

WASTING TIME

Time is something we all think we have plenty of. During the school year students think, "Will it ever be summer?" But we need to be good stewards of our time. We need to use our time wisely.

We need to spend time *alone* with God. I'm not talking about that five minutes every morning. I'm not even talking about that one hour every morning. I'm talking about a communion between you and God. You don't have to be like a monk and live up in the hills. You can be alone with God and still have your normal lifestyle by just getting rid of some things. We have so much busyness in our lives.

Turn off the television in the evenings. Turn off the radio in your car. Spend time by yourself in your room with no distractions. When it's quiet and you have nothing to distract your mind, you can hear that still small voice of the Holy Spirit. When God knows He has your undivided attention, He will impart wisdom and understanding to you. You will begin to grow and mature. You will begin to sharpen the edge.

We have been conditioned that we must always be doing something. If we're not in school, we must be at ball practice. If we're not at practice, we must be at work. And if we're not at work, we must be at home getting ourselves ready to start all over again the next day.

Have you ever had your electricity go out during a storm? It can get awfully quiet. No radio, no television, no telephone — you don't even hear the hum of the refrigerator. During those times we think, *What are we going to do?* There's nothing to watch, nothing to listen to, nothing to input into our brain. It's just very still and quiet. What do you do? Do you make it a family time where you just sit and talk? Do you take advantage of the quiet?

Don't wait for the electricity to go out and you're forced to be quiet before God. If you're waiting for that, you've probably lost the edge already! Commit to having that rich communion time with Him every day.

What steals your time from God?

_____

_____

_____

_____

What are you going to put aside to allow the Holy Spirit to speak to you?

_____

_____

_____

CHECKLIST:

• • • • • • • • • • • • •

- ☐ Today, read John 6.
- ☐ Is there any sin you need to repent of today?
- ☐ Are you grateful that God has forgiven you?
- ☐ Have you been talked out of any part of your Christianity?
- ☐ Will you give your all to Jesus today?
- ☐ Spend some time praising and worshipping God.
- ☐ Pray over your own life and your day today.
- ☐ Pray for your family, friends, and those in authority.
- ☐ Pray for the people of the world to be saved.
- ☐ Ask God if He wants you to go on a mission trip next summer.
- ☐ Do you have the edge to meet the challenges of your day?

HOW TO LOSE THE EDGE

Day 4

UNHEALED WOUNDS

"Come to me, all you who are weary and burdened, and I
will give you rest.
"Take my yoke upon you and learn from me, for I am gentle
and humble in heart, and you will find rest for your souls.
"For my yoke is easy and my burden is light."

Matthew 11:28-30

It's too bad we can't live in the Garden of Eden where everything was perfect — perfect weather, perfect food, perfect
animals, and perfect people. No, we live in the *real world*. Along
with the real world, we have real hurts and real pains that leave
real wounds. If we don't deal with those wounds, they will fester
on the inside of us and cause us to lose the edge.

There is so much hurt among young people today. Physical,
spiritual, and emotional abuses happen to too many young
children. Children are being beaten by their parents, sexually
abused by family members, and verbally ripped apart. Too

many suffer the horrible effects of divorce. It's a wonder any of them grow up to be halfway normal.

But they all learn to cope — one way or another — with their wounds. A rising number of teenagers suffer from eating disorders. We are seeing more and more violence in the nation's schools. Some run away from home, thinking anything would be better than what they are having to deal with at home. Then there are others who bury everything inside until they are adults and then spend the rest of their lives in a psychiatrist's office. Sadly, many of the wounded people in the world today are Christians. The worst thing is not that they have suffered pain, but that they have never been able to let Jesus heal their wounds.

You may be suffering from a wound yourself. It may not necessarily have come from a parent or a family member. Your pain might have come as a result of a boyfriend or girlfriend breakup. It might have come from a best friend who betrayed you or gossiped about you. But it doesn't matter where the wound came from. What matters is that you have the Answer.

You may be thinking, *Well, that can't possibly be me. Sure, I have been hurt in the past, but I'm okay now.*

Are you really?

If you see the person who hurt you, does your heart rate go up?

Do you suddenly relive the pain, and do you want to see that person hurt?

Are there times your heart still aches?

If you said yes to any of these questions, you haven't allowed Jesus to clean out that wound and heal it.

Unresolved past hurts can render you virtually ineffective for the kingdom of God, stunting your spiritual growth. But we have *the* only Answer — Jesus Christ.

The Spirit of the Lord is upon me, because he hath anointed me to preach the gospel to the poor; he hath sent

me to heal the brokenhearted, to preach deliverance to the captives, and recovering of sight to the blind, to set at liberty them that are bruised.

Luke 4:18 KJV

What hurts do you need to release to God? Write them down as an act of letting them go and turning them over to Jesus, your Healer. Then when you are reminded of them, tell the devil that you have been set free.

_____

_____

_____

_____

Ask the Lord to begin healing your broken heart and your wounded emotions. Pray a prayer of forgiveness for not letting go of that hurt and the memories that are trying to devour your future. Forgive those who have hurt you.

Once you let go of these hurts, never accept them again! The devil will try to convince you that you are not really healed, and he may even have someone come along and try to do the same thing to hurt you, but don't accept it! The only thing you will be accepting from now on is the healing power of Jesus!

CHECKLIST:

- [ ] Today, read John 7.
- [ ] Is there any sin you need to repent of today?
- [ ] Are you grateful that God has forgiven you?
- [ ] Have you been talked out of any part of your Christianity?
- [ ] Will you give your all to Jesus today?
- [ ] Spend some time praising and worshipping God.
- [ ] Pray over your own life and your day today.
- [ ] Pray for your family, friends, and those in authority.
- [ ] Pray for the people of the world to be saved.
- [ ] Ask God if He wants you to go on a mission trip next summer.
- [ ] Do you have the edge to meet the challenges of your day?

169

How to Lose the Edge

Day 5
● ●

LACK OF DISCIPLINE

Since, then, you have been raised with Christ, set your hearts on things above, where Christ is seated at the right hand of God.

Set your minds on things above, not on earthly things.

Colossians 3;1,2

Someone who has the edge is disciplined in both spiritual and physical matters. We think the only thing that matters is that we pray as much as we can and read our Bible every day. I'm not saying we should be robots in that we stick to a bunch of rules and regulations. But we're to be disciplined in seeking real life.

Being *disciplined* is putting God first in your life — in everything you do and say. It means you're pushing yourself to get into the Holy of Holies and get the real life. Being disciplined is reading the Bible because you know it is your source of faith and strength. Being disciplined is praying because you know that daily communion with the living God is the highlight of your day. Being disciplined is spending time praising and worshipping the Lord because you know praise stills the enemy.

Being *undisciplined* is self-centeredness — you read the Bible and pray when *you* feel like it. Your world revolves around you and no one else. Every decision you make is based on how it will benefit you. You don't have a heart of love and compassion for others. You may love people, but it's a conditional love — you'll love them as long as you're getting something from them. Being undisciplined is not seeing others how God sees them. This may come as a deep revelation to some, but Jesus died on the cross for *everyone!*

Therefore, as God's chosen people, holy and dearly loved, clothe yourselves with compassion, kindness, humility, gentleness and patience.

Bear with each other and forgive whatever grievances you may have against one another. Forgive as the Lord forgave you.

And over all these virtues put on love, which binds them all together in perfect unity.

Colossians 3:12-14

It's hard to believe that someone is really spiritually disciplined if they're not physically disciplined. Do you lead a disciplined lifestyle? That covers everything from the food you eat to what you do with your spare time.

I believe Christians should be examples of excellence. If you are an athlete, are you working as hard as you can to be the best you can? If you have a job, do you give your employer the best of your abilities? Do you show up for work on time and stay until it's time to leave? In school, do you take your education seriously? Do you strive to make the best grades possible or are you satisfied with just sliding by?

You may think, *What does all this have to do with anything?* How you answer these questions indicates whether or not you lead a disciplined lifestyle.

List four areas of your everyday life in which you need to be more disciplined.

1._____

2._____

3._____

4._____

List four ways you can be more spiritually disciplined.

CHECKLIST:

1. _____

_____

☐ Today, read John 8.

☐ Is there any sin you
need to repent of today?

2. _____

☐ Are you grateful that
God has forgiven you?

_____

3. _____

☐ Have you been talked
out of any part of your
Christianity?

_____

4. _____

☐ Will you give your all to
Jesus today?

_____

☐ Spend some time
praising and worship-
ping God.

☐ Pray over your own life
and your day today.

☐ Pray for your family,
friends, and those in
authority.

☐ Pray for the people of
the world to be saved.

☐ Ask God if He wants
you to go on a mission
trip next summer.

☐ Do you have the edge to
meet the challenges of
your day?

How to Lose the Edge

WEARINESS

Let us not become weary in doing good, for at the proper time we will reap a harvest if we do not give up.

Galatians 6:9

All the time I see people, young and old, who are frustrated with their Christian walk. They do all the right things — they read their Bible, they pray, they witness to their friends, they go on mission trips, they work in their youth group, and they volunteer whenever necessary. They work really hard, but they have begun to just go through the motions. Anything having to do with ministry has become *work*. And when all you do is *work*, you get very tired — you grow weary in doing good things. The least little thing becomes a burden.

If God is the source of their strength, why does this happen? It's because they're weary. They are operating without the edge. They are doing good things, but not as unto the Lord. Their passion and fire look more like a small lighted match because their whole focus is on how tired they are, how much they have done and are doing, and how little results and rewards they have gotten for all their work.

When your youth group goes out and witnesses to people, do you think, *Oh man, another night talking to a bunch of perverts about Jesus. Why don't they just get their life straightened out!* Or does your heart fill with excitement in anticipation of leading someone to Jesus? *Wow! I can't wait to share Jesus.*

What about your friends at school? Maybe there have been a few you have witnessed to many times without any response from them. You're so tired of them saying no that you've given up. You think, *If they haven't said yes to Jesus by now, they never will.* Or you have invited a friend to come to your youth group so many times that you've lost count. You think, *Why ask again? They'll just say no.*

These are *weary* responses! Wake up! You are losing the edge!

God has put something fresh and alive in you — the Holy Spirit — the same Spirit Who resurrected Jesus from the dead LIVES IN YOU!

You say, "I know that. So how do I wake up? How do I keep from growing weary in doing good things?"

And whatsoever ye do, do it heartily, as to the Lord, and not unto men;

Knowing that of the Lord ye shall receive the reward of the inheritance: for ye serve the Lord Christ.

Colossians 3:23,24 KJV

First, do everything as if Jesus was standing right next to you, asking you to do it. Whether it is helping your parents around the house, helping your brother or sister with their homework, taking the dog for a walk, witnessing to a friend, going to youth group, or going on a mission trip — you are doing it all for Jesus. If that is your attitude, you will not get tired of doing good.

Secondly, check your heart. What motivates you to do the good things you do? Do you want to be recognized? Are you promoting yourself or God? Do you want something in return? Or do you just want to please Jesus?

We were never meant to do anything for God without having the edge.

The Lord is the everlasting God, the Creator of the ends of the earth. He will not grow tired or weary, and his understanding no one can fathom.

He gives strength to the weary and increases the power of the weak.

Even youths grow tired and weary, and young men stumble and fall;

But those who hope in the Lord will renew their strength. They will soar on wings like eagles; they will run and not grow weary, they will walk and not be faint.

Isaiah 40:28-31

Write down any place you've gotten weary and have nearly given up. This could be a dream, a friend being saved, or your participation in youth group.

_____

_____

_____

_____

_____

Now declare, "God, I am not going to give up on the things I know You have called me to do. From now on I am going to look to You for my sole strength. I am going to do everything as if You were personally asking me to do it."

CHECKLIST:

☐ Today, read John 9 and 10.

☐ Is there any sin you need to repent of today?

☐ Are you grateful that God has forgiven you?

☐ Have you been talked out of any part of your Christianity?

☐ Will you give your all to Jesus today?

☐ Spend some time praising and worshipping God.

☐ Pray over your own life and your day today.

☐ Pray for your family, friends, and those in authority.

☐ Pray for the people of the world to be saved.

☐ Ask God if He wants you to go on a mission trip next summer.

☐ Do you have the edge to meet the challenges of your day?

How to Lose the Edge

Day 7

GETTING THE EDGE BACK

I want to know Christ and the power of his resurrection.

Not that I have already obtained all this, or have already been made perfect, but I press on to take hold of that for which Christ Jesus took hold of me.

Brothers, I do not consider myself yet to have taken hold of it. But one thing I do: Forgetting what is behind and straining toward what is ahead,

I press on toward the goal to win the prize for which God has called me heavenward in Christ Jesus.

Philippians 3:10,12-14

You may not have lived the most holy life. If they were to put a plaque up with the names of all the saints in your school, your name may not be on it. That's not important anymore. Paul wrote this passage of Scripture and he lived a very colorful life. He was a Pharisee before he had an encounter with Jesus. (See

Philippians 3:5.) He had persecuted the church, dragging Christians out of their homes and killing them for their faith. (See Philippians 3:6 and Acts 8:1-3.) He was there when Stephen was stoned to death. (See Acts 7:58.) Paul was a bad dude!

But when he had an encounter with the living God and committed his life completely to Jesus, he was a changed man. He went on to disciple many believers, ministered in many churches, started churches, and wrote much of the New Testament. He developed the edge *after* he did such horrible things, and you can too.

If you've lost the edge, you're just mediocre. You're in the middle of the crowd. You're no different from anyone else. You just kind of blend in. Your witness isn't very effective because no one notices. You can have lots of friends, a good social life, and look like you're fitting in, or you can go after the edge — you can get it back!

Separate yourself from the crowd and go into the Holy of Holies. Ask the Lord to show you what is preventing you from having the edge and repent. Cry out to Him and say, "God, I'm going for the gold. I want the Holy of Holies. I want what Elijah had. I want what David had. I want what Moses had. I want what Jacob had when he said, 'Give me that blessing!' I want what John the Baptist had. I want what Peter and Paul had. I want the edge, God!"

The edge separates you from the pack. You have more guts and more authority in Jesus Christ when you have the edge. You speak with power. You have a thunder in your voice because you have a raging fire going on inside you. You're confident of who you are. You're not looking for a title or making sure people are looking up to you. All that doesn't matter because you have the edge. You have God and that's all that matters.

Let your heart be open to whatever God wants to do in your life.

"For I know the plans I have for you," declares the Lord, "plans to prosper you and not to harm you, plans to give you hope and a future."

Jeremiah 29:11

Do you blend in with the crowd?

Are you willing to do whatever it takes to get the edge back?

CHECKLIST:

What plans do you think God has for you?

- ☐ Today, read John 11 and 12.
- ☐ Is there any sin you need to repent of today?

_____

_____

_____

- ☐ Are you grateful that God has forgiven you?

_____

What is preventing you from having the edge?

- ☐ Have you been talked out of any part of your Christianity?
- ☐ Will you give your all to Jesus today?

_____

_____

- ☐ Spend some time praising and worshipping God.

_____

_____

- ☐ Pray over your own life and your day today.
- ☐ Pray for your family, friends, and those in authority.
- ☐ Pray for the people of the world to be saved.
- ☐ Ask God if He wants you to go on a mission trip next summer.
- ☐ Do you have the edge to meet the challenges of your day?

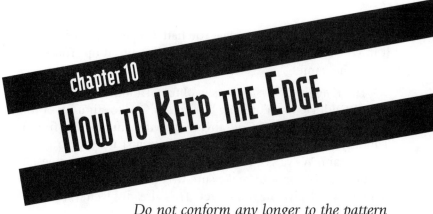

chapter 10

HOW TO KEEP THE EDGE

*Do not conform any longer to the pattern
of this world, but be transformed by the
renewing of your mind. Then you will be
able to test and approve what God's will is —
his good, pleasing and perfect will.*

Romans 12:2

Day 1

FANNING THE FLAME

**For this reason I remind you to fan into flame the gift of
God, which is in you through the laying on of my hands.**

**For God did not give us a spirit of timidity, but a spirit of
power, of love and of self-discipline.**

2 Timothy 1:6,7

This is a simple little scripture with a lot of power. Timothy
was a disciple of Paul who had gone on the missionary trail and
traveled with him. Paul had ministered to Timothy, discipled
him, raised him up, poured his life into him, laid his hands on
him, and sent him off into ministry.

Paul had invested so much in Timothy and knew him so
well, that when he began to see some problems he said,

"Timothy, you've lost the edge. You had it! I know you did. I saw it in you. Now Timothy, you need to stir yourself up. You need to fan the flame!"

The *King James Version* says Paul told Timothy to **stir up the gift of God.** He wasn't telling him to ask God to stir it up or for God to fan the flame. God already put the gift and the fire in Timothy, but it was dying down and he just needed to get it going again. We've got to work at making sure our fire doesn't die down. We've got to make sure we don't get stale. We're not to pray, "Lord, give me more fire!" He's already given us the fire! He's already placed the gift within us.

I remember learning how to light the charcoal fire on the barbecue when I was a teenager. Now when my dad or mom did it, it looked real easy. I thought, "You just squirt the lighter fluid on the coals and light them." So I would squirt the stuff on, light it, and expect to go out there in about a half hour and find glowing coals. But when I'd go back out and check it, it was dead.

"Well, I better light it again." So I'd squirt the stuff on, light it again, come out in a half hour — still not lit. "Stupid thing, what's wrong with this stuff? I know it was raging when I left." So I'd keep squirting and lighting, squirting and lighting.

Are we like that? "Whoo, we've got the fire! Boy, did we have church!" for about ten seconds after service. Then we go home, turn on the TV, and by the next day we wonder what's happened. Paul said, "You gotta *fan* that flame."

After years of practice, I know I need to blow some air on that charcoal or fan it to keep it going and make it stronger and stronger and hotter and hotter. I used to think, *You blow on fire and it'll put it out.* After all, you blow on a match and it goes out, so why not the whole thing? But on the contrary, when you blow on it the oxygen feeds the fire.

You don't ever want to put your meat on the grill until those coals are glowing red hot. If you put the meat on there before it's glowing hot, the fire will probably go out. Then your food is halfway done and if you try to fan the flame, you just get ashes all over the place. It's pretty nasty!

I wonder if that's how we are sometimes. We go through the Christian life sort of half-lit. Then when we find ourselves in a desperate situation we say, "Oh God, please make up for all the times I didn't pray or read my Bible," and we blow and blow and ashes start going everywhere. Does that sound like you?

We need to be passionately fanning those coals until they're hot and glowing — till we have a raging fire — and then keep fanning them. Then we've got the edge. We don't have just a little bit of an experience, we've got a glowing, inner-fervor that will not die. And people will see it in our eyes, our countenance, and our lifestyle.

How do you do this? Pray without ceasing and listen to the Holy Spirit at all times, especially when it comes to developing the gifts and talents — spiritual and natural — God has given you. The Holy Spirit is that mighty rushing wind who keeps the fire burning. He's the One who shows you what to do and when with those gifts and talents. Sticking close to Him is a major key to keeping the edge

Go for the glow!

What gifts has God placed inside of you that you need to stir up?

_____

_____

_____

_____

CHECKLIST:
· · · · · · · · · · · · · · ·

☐ Today read John 13.

☐ Is there any sin you need to repent of today?

☐ Are you grateful that God has forgiven you?

☐ Have you been talked out of any part of your Christianity?

☐ Will you give your all to Jesus today?

☐ Spend some time praising and worshipping God.

☐ Pray over your own life and your day today.

☐ Pray for your family, friends, and those in authority.

☐ Pray for the people of the world to be saved.

☐ Ask God if He wants you to go on a mission trip next summer.

☐ Do you have the edge to meet the challenges of your day?

How to Keep the Edge

Day 2
● ●

COMMUNION WITH GOD

The grace of the Lord Jesus Christ, and the love of God, and the communion of the Holy Ghost, be with you all. Amen.

2 Corinthians 13:14

Prayer is communion, or connecting, with God. I wonder how many people pray and never connect. How many people go through the rituals and never really have communion? To keep the edge sharp, we must connect with God.

The opposite of a sharp edge is a dull edge. We don't want a dull edge! Unless you keep it sharpened through prayer, the edge will become dull. What can you do with a dull edge? Not much! You can saw away for hours and not cut anything!

Some knives are advertised as never having to be sharpened. I bought one thinking, *Man this is great — a knife I'll never have to sharpen. It must be made out of some supernatural steel or something.* But now it won't even cut butter! I try to cut bread with it and it hacks it all up. It makes me so mad that I bought such a stupid piece of junk. They're guaranteed, but who keeps the guarantee paper on a three-dollar knife?

● ● ● ●

That's how Christians are sometimes. We think there's some sort of guarantee that we'll never go dull. There is no guarantee! You have to sharpen the edge — pray — every day. The sad thing is, some of us are dull and don't know it. So we go through our day and we start hacking away. Hack! Hack! Hack! We're trying to cut through our day with a dull edge. We think, *What's wrong with this knife? I can't believe this is so difficult!* There's nothing wrong with the knife — the edge just isn't sharp. We didn't start our day out with prayer. We haven't had communion with God and committed everything to Him. We need to sharpen the edge.

Another thing about a knife: If you start beating it on a rock, after awhile it will get dull. Every once in a while you might be able to cut something, but for the most part the knife is all beat up. But if you'll stop, lay the knife on its side, and start filing it back and forth on that hard surface, the edge of the knife will be sharpened.

So many times we want to just hack our way through the hard challenges we face. But if we'll say, "Wait a minute. I'm gonna let this thing sharpen me. I'm gonna start praying. I'm going to find the real answer to this problem. I'm gonna pray until I've got a word from God." Then, BOOM! We've just cut through the hardness.

Let your challenges push you to sharpen you. When you sharpen yourself, you keep the edge!

List your most pressing prayer requests — the hardest things you're facing right now — and take time to pray until God speaks to you about them.

_____

CHECKLIST:
• • • • • • • • • • • • •

☐ Today, read John 14.

☐ Is there any sin you need to repent of today?

☐ Are you grateful that God has forgiven you?

☐ Have you been talked out of any part of your Christianity?

☐ Will you give your all to Jesus today?

☐ Spend some time praising and worshipping God.

☐ Pray over your own life and your day today.

☐ Pray for your family, friends, and those in authority.

☐ Pray for the people of the world to be saved.

☐ Ask God if He wants you to go on a mission trip next summer.

☐ Do you have the edge to meet the challenges of your day?

How to Keep the Edge

Day 3

FASTING

To fast means to abstain from food altogether or certain types of food for a specified time. We don't hear a lot said about fasting today. A lot of people think, *Fasting, that's just for old folks and ministers and monks.* People don't normally shout and scream when they hear a message on fasting!

"When you fast, do not look somber as the hypocrites do, for they disfigure their faces to show men they are fasting. I tell you the truth, they have received their reward in full.

"But when you fast, put oil on your head and wash your face,

"So that it will not be obvious to men that you are fasting, but only to your Father, who is unseen; and your Father, who sees what is done in secret, will reward you."

Matthew 6:16-18

Notice it says, *when* you fast, not *if* you fast. Jesus expects us to fast. He didn't instruct His disciples, "If you get around to it and if you're really superspiritual, try fasting." He expects us to make it part of our lifestyle. And it's not something we need to let the entire school know about. When you fast, get yourself washed up and keep it private between you and the Lord. Your Father will reward you.

Why do we fast? Fasting sharpens you. It humbles you. It gets you crying out to God. When you are denying your body of things it craves every day in order to get direction from God, scriptures are illuminated to you like never before. The Holy Spirit will give you the specific answer for the problem that seems impossible to solve. You separate yourself from the world and say, "Lord, I don't want the bread of this world. I want the bread that comes from heaven."

Fasting is not just going hungry. Some people go through the motions of fasting, but they don't get anything out of it. "Well, I just fasted for three days." If your goal was not to eat, then that's what you did. But fasting means feasting on the bread from above. You're telling God, "I'm coming after You with everything in me. Lord, I'm getting away from the things of this world and putting my entire attention on You like never before."

I want to give you one word of warning. If you are planning a prolonged fast, please get your doctor's permission first. Teens are still growing and need lots of nutrients. If it is not physically safe for you to completely fast all food, you can fast certain foods that you especially like, such as sweets and soda pop.

Sometimes a fast can be one of the hardest things to do. You have to be determined! But with Holy Ghost determination, nothing will stop you and you will not only keep the edge, you will increase the anointing on your life.

Have you ever fasted?

List three things you need answers for that may come only by fasting.

1._____

_____

2._____

_____

3._____

_____

_____

CHECKLIST:

☐ Today, read John 15.

☐ Is there any sin you need to repent of today?

☐ Are you grateful that God has forgiven you?

☐ Have you been talked out of any part of your Christianity?

☐ Will you give your all to Jesus today?

☐ Spend some time praising and worshipping God.

☐ Pray over your own life and your day today.

☐ Pray for your family, friends, and those in authority.

☐ Pray for the people of the world to be saved.

☐ Ask God if He wants you to go on a mission trip next summer.

☐ Do you have the edge to meet the challenges of your day?

How to Keep the Edge

Day 4

MEDITATING ON THE WORD

For all flesh [mankind] is like grass and all its glory (honor) like [the] flower of grass. The grass withers, and the flower drops off.

But the Word of the Lord (divine instruction, the Gospel) endures forever. And this Word is the good news which was preached to you.

1 Peter 1:24,25 AMP

This Scripture tells us that God's Word will last forever. The clothes we own, the cars we drive, the houses we live in, and even our physical bodies will die away, but God's Word stands forever. To keep the edge, we must meditate in God's Word every day.

There are so many different ways of studying Scripture. You can study the lives of people in the Bible, such as Paul, Timothy, or David. You can study different topics the Bible addresses, such as salvation, grace, forgiveness, healing, or submission to authority.

Another very powerful key is to memorize Scripture. That might be a new concept for you. You probably haven't done that since Vacation Bible School, but a raging fire not only needs oxygen; it needs wood. And the Word of God is your fuel. By memorizing and meditating on Scripture, you give the fire more fuel to burn hotter and brighter.

One thing I encourage you to do is to look for the character of God in Scripture. This is how you really get to know Him, what His character is. Think about your friends. You have those who are just an acquaintance. You know each other, greet each other in the hallways, you may even sit by them in class or on the bus. But they're not your *best friend*. You don't share your deepest thoughts, hopes, and dreams with them. You don't really *know* them.

When you have a really good friend, you know them very well. If someone accuses them of doing wrong, you could say, "No, no, no. They'd never do that. I *know* them." Is it because you just know their name? No. It's because you know their character and personality. So how did you get to know them so well? Wasn't it by spending lots and lots of time with them, doing things together, and just sitting around talking about things?

Sometimes we talk about getting to know the Lord, but it seems like we're just grabbing the air! Do you know what God's like? Do you know His personality, His character, and His nature? Do you spend lots of time studying His Word, praying, and talking and communing with Him?

You meditate on the Word because you are on a quest to know God! When you read the Bible, always say, "God, show me Your character. Explain to me what You're like, what You don't like, and what You do like. I want to *know* You!" Getting to know Him is getting to know His character.

As you read your Bible, think about what God did, what He said, and why He did and said those things. He reveals Himself through Scripture. His character is not meant to be a deep, dark secret. He *wants* us to know Him. And when you read about Jesus, He said, "If you've seen Me, you've seen the Father." (See

John 14:9.) What you see in Jesus is what God is like.

Meditating and studying God's Word lets you know God, and that gives you the edge. The Word brings you life and you know it'll bring someone else life too!

How much time do you spend studying the Word of God?

_____

_____

List three things you want to study in the Bible.

1. _____

2. _____

3. _____

CHECKLIST:

☐ Today, read John 16.

☐ Is there any sin you need to repent of today?

☐ Are you grateful that God has forgiven you?

☐ Have you been talked out of any part of your Christianity?

☐ Will you give your all to Jesus today?

☐ Spend some time praising and worshipping God.

☐ Pray over your own life and your day today.

☐ Pray for your family, friends, and those in authority.

☐ Pray for the people of the world to be saved.

☐ Ask God if He wants you to go on a mission trip next summer.

☐ Do you have the edge to meet the challenges of your day?

HOW TO KEEP THE EDGE

Day 5
•••••••••••••••••••••••

CREATIVE QUIET TIMES

As the deer pants for streams of water, so my soul pants for you, O God.

Psalm 42:1

We need to study the Word of God, pray, and spend time praising and worshipping God during our quiet times. Sometimes we get in a rut and do the same thing the same way every day, and it can get boring. If you're bored with something, you're less likely to do it. We can have creative times with God so our quiet time doesn't get boring, but rather it stays fresh and new. You'll have fresh embers and fresh coals to put on your fire in different ways.

First of all, pray for different things. Don't just go down your prayer list, "I pray for this, and this, and this. Whew, I'm done! I'm outta here!" Pray specifically, and pray for things that don't necessarily benefit you. Pray for God to bless other people. Pray for someone else's ministry, someone else's youth group, someone else's church, and someone else's problems.

You'll be amazed at what will begin to happen in your own life when your prayer time consists of more than your little wish list. It's a time to get to know God and let Him stir your heart for others.

Secondly, have creative times of worship. To me, worship is the essence of our encounter with God.

Enter his gates with thanksgiving and his courts with praise; give thanks to him and praise his name.

Psalm 100:4

There's only one way to get into the courts of the Lord, and that's with thanksgiving and praise. It's not by offering a sacrifice of goats and lambs, but by the sacrifice of praise. Before Jesus came, the only way the priests could enter the Holy of Holies was to offer certain animal sacrifices. But Jesus is our sacrifice. The work He did on the cross was done so we could enter into God's presence wherever and whenever we want.

Have sincere times of creative worship. Don't ever sing a song for the sake of singing a song. Don't let it just come out of your lips and not from your heart. Sing songs that stir your heart and inspire your soul — and sing them to Jesus. Take some of the Psalms and read them to the Father like you wrote them to Him.

I can't wait for a worship service in heaven. Revelation 4 tells us about the twenty-four elders on their faces before the throne of God. They are so stunned by God's presence, they can't even stand up. They're so awestruck they can't say anything but, "Holy, holy, holy..." for the first million years!

Find ways to study the Word of God differently. It's like we talked about yesterday — you can study topics, themes, and people, but your ultimate goal is to find out who God is and what His character is. If you don't know what to study, ask the Lord to show you.

List three things you have *never* prayed about before.

1._____

2._____

3._____

What songs are really captivating your heart today? Sing them to Jesus.

_____

_____

CHECKLIST:
• • • • • • • • • • • • • •

☐ Today, read John 17.

☐ Is there any sin you need to repent of today?

☐ Are you grateful that God has forgiven you?

☐ Have you been talked out of any part of your Christianity?

☐ Will you give your all to Jesus today?

☐ Spend some time praising and worshipping God.

☐ Pray over your own life and your day today.

☐ Pray for your family, friends, and those in authority.

☐ Pray for the people of the world to be saved.

☐ Ask God if He wants you to go on a mission trip next summer.

☐ Do you have the edge to meet the challenges of your day?

_____

_____

List three Bible topics you have never studied. Then pick one to study.

1. _____

2. _____

3. _____

How to Keep the Edge

Day 6
. . . .

Set Personal Goals

To keep the edge, you need to set some personal goals. What kind of a man or woman of God do you want to be? Some Christians say, "Well, I just want to be like Jesus. I just want to have God's presence all over my life." Good! Now how does that translate in practical terms?

Set personal goals. Think about what you want to be like in six months, a year, and five years from now. Then make plans to accomplish that. Figure out what it's going to take to get you there. Maybe you are in high school right now and you want to be in college in five years. You need to begin asking God to show you where He wants you to go, checking the colleges and universities out, and seeing what they have to offer. Don't wait until the day you graduate to say, "College? Oh yeah, that's what I want to do."

Some of your personal goals can be things like, "I want to read a certain number of books. I want to read through the Bible a certain number of times. I want to spend a certain amount of time praying each day." They can also be the results you want to have, not just things you want to do. Set your goals in terms of results, then find out the things you need to do to get those results.

Put together a wish list with a very specific and realistic set of goals. "I want to have the compassion of Jesus." A lot of times we set goals that are way out there like, "I want to fast every Friday for the rest of my life and have an all-night prayer meeting three times a week." Then we feel bad and hit ourselves over the head when we can't fulfill them. So set some realistic goals and decide you're going to do them, whatever it takes.

After setting goals, we often come up with excuses why we can't fulfill them. Don't let that hinder you anymore. If you need a new Bible to study, then go buy one. If you need some study tools, such as other books and tapes, go get them. But if you're going to spend the money on these things, make sure you use them. Don't buy all this stuff and then let it sit in a closet collecting dust!

Americans are nuts for setting goals, getting the stuff to help them, then not following through. YOU'VE GOT TO HAVE FOLLOW-THROUGH! At the beginning of every year, people make resolutions to exercise, get in shape, and lose weight. They spend tons of money on health spas, fitness clubs, and home exercise equipment. They think, *I'm really committed, because I'm spending this money.* For the most part, it lasts a few weeks, or maybe even a few months. But by the time September rolls around, most of the exercise equipment just sits in a room unused.

It's the same thing when you set spiritual goals. You can have all the Bibles, books, and tapes you can think of, but unless you use them, it won't do you a bit of good. When you set a goal, set your face like flint, go for the long haul, and make it happen! Then you will keep the edge!

List three small goals you want to accomplish.

1._____

2._____

3._____

How do you plan to make them happen?

_____

_____

_____

_____

List three big goals you want to accomplish.

1. _____

2. _____

3. _____

How do you plan to make them happen?

_____

_____

_____

_____

_____

_____

_____

_____

_____

_____

_____

_____

_____

CHECKLIST:

☐ Today, read John 18 and 19.

☐ Is there any sin you need to repent of today?

☐ Are you grateful that God has forgiven you?

☐ Have you been talked out of any part of your Christianity?

☐ Will you give your all to Jesus today?

☐ Spend some time praising and worshipping God.

☐ Pray over your own life and your day today.

☐ Pray for your family, friends, and those in authority.

☐ Pray for the people of the world to be saved.

☐ Ask God if He wants you to go on a mission trip next summer.

☐ Do you have the edge to meet the challenges of your day?

How to Keep the Edge

Day 7

CHANGING THE WORLD

As Christians, we're in full-time ministry every second of the day. We're called to spread the Gospel.

You will affect the people closest to you, such as your family and friends, but you may feel called to be one of the ministry gifts listed in Ephesians 4:11: an apostle, prophet, evangelist, pastor, or teacher — to go out into the world.

Start where you are right now. I hear young people say, "Well, I would witness to my friends, but I really feel called to Russia." God may have called you overseas, but right now He has planted you at your school, in your community, and with your friends for a reason. Prove yourself faithful today so God can send you out tomorrow.

You don't have to wait until you're an adult to minister either. Maybe you feel you're too young and don't know much about the Lord. Maybe you feel like you don't really have the edge just yet. Sometimes you walk around acting like you don't have anything between your ears, but that's okay! God can use you *if* you are willing. He's not looking for someone with great talent or someone who has the Bible memorized. He's looking for someone just like you — willing to change the world by obeying His Word and Spirit.

More and more teenagers are going on mission trips each year. More and more teens are saying, "I'm tired of my world revolving around *me*. I want to prefer others, give myself away, and be selfless for the Gospel of Jesus Christ. I want to see lives drastically changed." Is that what you are thinking also?

Peter said to him, "We have left everything to follow you!"

"I tell you the truth," Jesus replied, "no one who has left home or brothers or sisters or mother or father or children or fields for me and the gospel will fail to receive a hundred times as much in this present age (homes, brothers, sisters, mothers, children and fields — and with them, persecutions) and in the age to come, eternal life."

Mark 10:28-30

When I felt the Lord wanted me to be in the ministry, I remember praying, "God, I don't want to be just another preacher. There's lots of preachers! Preachers on the radio, preachers on TV, preachers doing this, preachers doing that — just another preacher?" God spoke to my heart, "Don't be just another preacher."

What makes you different is having the edge. You are radical about the Gospel and radical for Jesus. You want more than anything in the world to see people's hearts turned towards God and changed forever.

You can spend time learning strategies, plans, and programs, but without the edge, you have nothing. Whether you minister in this nation or overseas, if you don't have the edge you'll just have a lot of activity without real ministry. I believe God wants us to have a Holy Ghost determination to go after the edge like Jacob did, "Don't You dare leave until You bless me! I can't let You leave until You bless me!"

Do you feel called to minister outside of your school and your community?

Is there a part of the world you feel drawn to? If so, where?

_____

What are you doing to prepare? Are you learning the culture and the language?

CHECKLIST:
• • • • • • • • • • • • • •

☐ Today, read John 20 and 21.

☐ Is there any sin you need to repent of today?

☐ Are you grateful that God has forgiven you?

☐ Have you been talked out of any part of your Christianity?

☐ Will you give your all to Jesus today?

☐ Spend some time praising and worshipping God.

☐ Pray over your own life and your day today.

☐ Pray for your family, friends, and those in authority.

☐ Pray for the people of the world to be saved.

☐ Ask God if He wants you to go on a mission trip next summer.

☐ Do you have the edge to meet the challenges of your day?

_____
_____
_____
_____

How are you spreading the Gospel in your school and community?

_____
_____
_____
_____

Conclusion

It's time for you to stand up and do your part in order for your generation to revolutionize this world for Jesus Christ! You can't rely on your parents, your friends, or even your church to get connected with Jesus and keep the edge. Yes, being active in church, hanging around good Christian friends, and having family prayer and Bible study will help. But you must keep your relationship with Jesus Christ new and fresh every day and refuse to be affected by people, emotions, ideas, or situations that would try to draw you away from God.

You're not going to be just an *average* Christian. You're going to be a *radical* Christian. You know God has called you to be different. He has separated you for His divine purpose and plan. He has called you to show the world the treasure — Jesus — who is inside of you. God has given you every tool you need to accomplish this: spiritual and natural gifts, callings, the measure of faith, and the power and authority of the Holy Spirit and the Word.

No longer are you going to go back and forth from being a mental Christian to an on-the-edge Christian, because you've experienced Jesus in a very real way. You've had to ask yourself some very serious and sometimes painful questions over the past ten weeks. I hope you answered each question honestly and poured your heart out to God. If you have, then you can now say, "Jesus is REAL. I've committed every part of my being to Him. I thank God I am forgiven, and I commit my life to serve Him and defeat sin, the devil, and all worldliness. My passion to reach the world is burning ballistic and I'M LIVING ON THE EDGE FOR JESUS!

About the Author

Ron Luce is president and CEO of Teen Mania Ministries, a national youth ministry based in Garden Valley, Texas, where they have built a campus to train teenagers to change the world. Teen Mania Global Expeditions takes young people overseas on short-term missions projects. In the summer of 1997, nearly 3,000 teenagers went to 19 different countries and saw over 122,000  people come to know the Lord. As of 1997, they had visited 35 different countries and witnessed over 384,000 people give their lives to Jesus. They also disciple and train teens through their one-year Teen Mania Honor Academy.

Ron Luce hosts "Acquire the Fire" youth conventions across the country. Over 130,000 teenagers are reached each year through these conventions, which consist of a weekend of radical Christian living with mammoth video walls, a live worship band, comedic sketches, and pyrotechnics. His "Acquire the Fire" weekly television program can be seen on Trinity Broadcasting Network.

Ron has appeared on the "700 Club," TBN, and Dr. James Dobson's "Focus on the Family" radio broadcast. He is the worship leader on four Teen Mania worship albums. Ron has been a guest speaker at chapel services in Christian colleges across America and at many youth conventions, including Kenneth Hagin's Campmeeting, Youth America, Youth for the Nations, and Washington for Jesus.

Raised in a broken home and suffering from several years of drug and alcohol abuse, Ron ran away from home at the age of fifteen before finding Jesus Christ at age sixteen. He went on to receive his Bachelor of Arts in Psychology and Theology from Oral Roberts University and his Master of Arts in Counseling Psychology from the University of Tulsa. Ron and his wife, Katie, have three children: Hannah, Charity, and Cameron.

Books by Ron Luce

Rescue Manual for Parents

*Mature Christians Are Boring People...And
Other Myths About Maturity in Christ*

*R.I.O.T. Manual
(co-authored with Carman)*

Inspire the Fire

56 Days Ablaze

Quit Playing with Fire

10 Challenges of a WorldChanger

Mark of a WorldChanger

To contact Ron Luce or Teen Mania Ministries,
please write:

P. O. Box 2000

Garden Valley, Texas 75771-2000

Additional copies of this book and other book titles
from ALBURY PUBLISHING are available at your local bookstore.

ALBURY PUBLISHING
P. O. Box 470406
Tulsa, Oklahoma 74147-0406

In Canada books are available from:
Word Alive
P. O. Box 670
Niverville, Manitoba
CANADA ROA 1EO